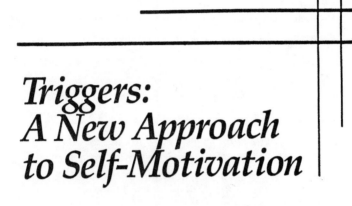

Triggers:
A New Approach
to Self-Motivation

Stanley Mann, A.C.S.W.

PRENTICE-HALL, INC.
ENGLEWOOD CLIFFS, NEW JERSEY 07632

Prentice-Hall International, Inc., *London*
Prentice-Hall of Australia, Pty. Ltd., *Sydney*
Prentice-Hall Canada, Inc., *Toronto*
Prentice-Hall of India Private Ltd., *New Delhi*
Prentice-Hall of Japan, Inc., *Tokyo*
Prentice-Hall of Southeast Asia Pte. Ltd., *Singapore*
Whitehall Books, Ltd., Wellington, *New Zealand*
Editora Prentice-Hall do Brasil Ltda., *Rio de Janeiro*
Prentice-Hall Hispanoamericana, S.A., *Mexico*

Copyright © 1987 by Stanley Mann

Fourth Printing . . . . . November 1987

Library of Congress Catalog Number: 86-063256

ISBN 0-13-930785-0

ISBN 0-13-930793-1 {PBK}

Printed in the United States of America

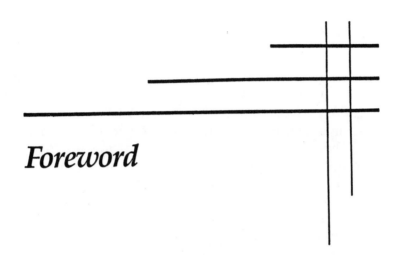

Foreword

We are in the midst of an exponential explosion in the number of people seeking psychological self-help methods to improve their life. They want to learn ways to achieve freedom from fear, better health, or success in life.

Self-help has many advantages. You can better yourself at your own time and pace, it is inexpensive, and it makes you self-reliant, which is the foundation of self-confidence.

Until recently, powerful psychological methods of improving human personality and increasing personal effectiveness have been the private domain of a handful of professionals. But the great secrets of quick, effective personality enhancement have been carefully gleaned from the esoteric professional literature by Mr. Mann. In this book, he makes these mental programming methods available, in the form of self-help, to all who are willing to invest a little time and energy to use them. Now you can share in these secrets.

The Trigger technique, from which this book's title is drawn, is a special kind of conditioned reflex, sometimes called an anchor. It is a powerful psychological tool for instantly accessing the mental resources lying within you.

By combining Triggers with such mental self-help methods as visualization, relaxation, and mental rehearsal, exceptionally powerful mind programming systems are made. These programming systems are tailor-made to achieve specific results. This enables Triggers' techniques to go much further than just visualization, mental rehearsal, or even self-hypnosis. And this is what makes *Triggers* different from other self-help books.

There is an old folk saying: Talking to a hungry man about food does not satisfy his hunger, giving him food feeds him only once, but if you teach him to raise his own crops, you feed him for the rest of his life. This is the essence of self-help.

This is Mr. Mann's goal: to teach you, the general reader, how to help yourself. He doesn't just talk in vague generalities about improving yourself, nor does he try to do it for you. Instead, he does a masterful job of translating the private language of researchers—a language that only a few can understand—to explain clearly and straightforwardly how mental programming works and how you can use it to enrich your life.

Great thinkers, like Newton and Einstein, explore the rarefied atmosphere of theory. They need practical men, in the tradition of people like Edison, to bring the benefits of the mysteries they have unraveled to the general public.

Mr. Mann uses his talents in the service of such a practical tradition. By translating this new psychological technology into readily learnable, and, therefore, practical terms, Mr. Mann completely fulfills his goal. Along with explicit instructions and simplified outlines, this book is filled with examples taken from his work with hundreds of patients and students. These examples clearly illustrate the methods he discusses, and are valuable for making the methods easy to learn and apply.

I have had the pleasure of a long professional association with Mr. Mann. We have been colleagues at the Veterans Administration, as well as in our private practice, for over eighteen years. Working as co-therapists, we have enjoyed unraveling many knotty problems that confront us in our work. I have also enjoyed leading professional workshops with him. Therefore, I have had the opportunity to observe him in many settings as a warmly intuitive therapist and remarkably effective teacher, trainer and facilitator.

My own years of experience with the methods he discusses in this book have shown me that they are astonishingly effective. I am sure they will give the reader the means to liberate himself from many common emotional blocks, as well as help him develop and use inner resources that may have been, until now, only dimly realized.

Ned Papania, Ph.D.
Past Director of Psychological Training
Veterans Administration Medical Center
Allen Park, Michigan

Director and Chief Psychologist
The Arbor Clinical Group
Detroit and Birmingham, Michigan

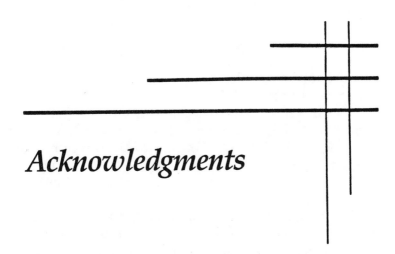

Acknowledgments

Whatever pride I may take in my accomplishments has to be taken with the full realization that nothing would have come to fruition without careful pruning, generous fertilization, and debugging by my many teachers, mentors, therapists, clients, family and friends.

The most profound investment was by my wife, who sacrificed her own career to cast her lot entirely with mine, so she could devote full time to smoothing the path for me. And sometimes I have asked her to help me along on some pretty rough paths. She has been unstintingly generous in sharing me with her two arch rivals: my work and my fishing. My writing this book has been possible only with her continuing forbearance. Her encouragement has meant, and still does mean, more to me than she may realize. It feels good to be able to state this publicly.

I have the good fortune to have as my professional mentor, Ned Papania, Ph.D., Director of Psychological Training at the Veterans Administration. A man of practical wisdom, he can cut through the nonsense of life and get to the essence of the matter. He has shared his extensive professional knowledge most generously with me. Sometimes I blush at the extent to which, driven by an avid curiosity, I have imposed on him. When reviewing my manuscript before the final editing, he gave many valuable suggestions to make this book more accurate and helpful.

Although I have received considerable professional training from many skillful people, I have benefited greatly from the teachings of William Q. Wolfson, M.D., director of the Metropolitan Transactional Analysis and Gestalt Institute in Livonia, Michigan. He also made some excellent suggestions when I was writing the manuscript.

Victoria Diaz, writer and teacher, has my deep appreciation for encouraging my plans to write this book, making editorial suggestions, and advising me on how to get published.

My thanks to David Wright for realizing the potential of Triggers in its early stages, and to Nancy Brandwein for her tireless efforts in helping me whip the book into its present form so that it was sensibly organized, told a logical story, made its concepts clear and conveyed the essential information. Nancy helped me reduce the book to the essential information and put the right emphasis on what the book can do for the reader. Her advice was invaluable.

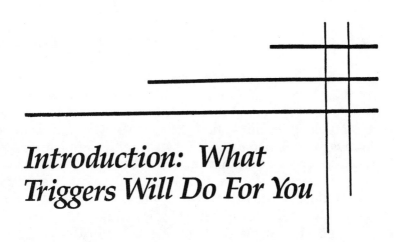

Introduction: What Triggers Will Do For You

In all areas of science, phenomenal gains in knowledge are creating dramatic breakthroughs. Space flight, computers, human organ transplants, telecommunications and genetic engineering are just some of the modern wonders of science benefiting us today.

Equally dramatic breakthroughs in personal improvement techniques are being made in psychology. This book tells you how to use the most up-to-date self-improvement technology known to science: mental programming, a psychological system for installing new capabilities and talents in yourself. It does this by improving the way you think, act, and react.

Central to these new mental programming methods is the *Trigger*—a spectacular breakthrough technique. Combining Triggers with new, improved imagery techniques has enabled scientists to design strikingly powerful self-improvement methods. These make it surprisingly easy to achieve the improvements needed for success.

HOW I FIRST LEARNED OF THESE NEW TECHNIQUES

When I returned home after my first professional seminar on these new techniques, my mind was in a whirl. I almost hadn't gone because I thought I had seen everything. After all, my previous training had covered Gestalt and Transactional Analysis, psychoanalysis, behavior modification, and sensitivity training. But the seminar turned out to have been an extremely exciting five days for me. Enabling people to realize their greater potential had always been fun for me and now I had a whole new set of powerful tools to help people with.

I became increasingly impressed with the power of these new techniques as I used them with my clients. Usually a client would make an astonishingly quick improvement and make gains that had previously taken months of tedious work using older methods. Now I could help someone improve (like the timid woman mentioned earlier) much easier and quicker.

In just four sessions, for instance, an aspiring executive gained all the action-packed motivation she needed to change her career. After three sessions, a war veteran, suffering recurrent combat nightmares, was able to sleep peacefully again. After two sessions, a salesman dramatically increased his confidence and soon became a star salesman. In just twenty minutes, a timid young woman became able to talk to anyone effectively—from an imposing judge to attractive men she wanted to meet. Such results used to take months or even years.

A REVOLUTIONARY IMPROVEMENT

As pleased as I was with these results, I began to wonder if a further advance could be made. These powerful methods of personal growth had been, virtually, the private property of a select group of professionals. They used them to help their clients change, but they reached only a small portion of the population. Not everyone has the money, time, or inclination to go to a professional.

How could these mind programming techniques, which could benefit practically everyone, be made available to more people?

I wondered if these new techniques would work if one applied them to oneself. If so, people could learn how to use them themselves. This would make these techniques widely available at a greatly reduced cost. More people could gain greater power over their lives and further their self-reliance and independence.

I decided to start testing out if it could be done. My first client was to be me. I chose to change something easy to measure, so I could tell what results I got. But something not too easy to change, so I could tell how powerful the technique was. I chose stopping smoking. It was something I wanted to do but had never been able to accomplish.

So I sat down and went through the steps I had been taught. I used an ingenious technique (which is explained in detail later in the book) that programs different parts of your personality to help change your bad habit. It took less than twenty minutes to complete, and when I was through, I wondered if it would work.

I soon discovered just how well it did work. When I reached for my cigarettes, a mental signal that I had programmed during my session told me to stop. What a happy surprise! My arm stopped in midair. From then on, the signal worked every time I even thought of getting a cigarette. I was impressed and delighted at how well these techniques worked as self-help. (By the way, I haven't smoked since.)

I knew then, since I was able to use these new methods to program myself, that my patients and others could use these techniques, too.

I was excited by the enormous possibilities this opened up. In my mind, being able to stop smoking wasn't all that earth shattering, even if the method of accomplishing it was delightfully easy and effective. What I was excited about was realizing that others could apply these easy and powerful methods *themselves* to improve *all* areas of their lives: behavioral, emotional, intellectual, and physical.

HOW YOU CAN USE TRIGGERS

When I began teaching my clients and students how to use these as self-help techniques, many asked for written instructions or books on the subject. I could only refer them to technical books and journals cloaked from the average reader by thick technical jargon. Furthermore, they were written for professionals to use on their clients, not to use on yourself. What was needed were instructions written in a straightforward manner which could be followed by anyone to use on him or herself.

Also, it occurred to me that such a book could reach a wide audience and let a great many people benefit from Triggers' mental programming techniques.

As a result, this book was written to explain these extremely useful methods from a self-help viewpoint.

Triggers does not just give you intellectual understanding or "insight." Exact methods are given to make the specific changes you want. Scientific jargon is stripped off and replaced with clear, everyday language. I include easy to follow, step-by-step instructions, and detailed examples of how others have used these techniques to immeasurably enrich their lives. Here are just a few of these masterful techniques and what they can do for you:

Breakthrough Technique #1— "The Trigger"

A few minutes is all it takes for you to create a "trigger"—the powerful mental reflex that is the foundation for all mental programming techniques in this guide. Your personal triggers will activate your hidden powers of motivation instantly so you can fulfill your every goal and desire. Many people have used this trigger reflex to finally accomplish things they'd only dreamed of doing for years. Whether you want to market your creative talents, make a difficult career move or even go on a diet, when you use your "trigger" you'll never have to push yourself to do the job—instead, you'll have to remind yourself to stop!

Breakthrough Technique #2—"The Mental Blueprint"

Now you can master new skills and challenges using the same technique Olympic champions have used to insure peak performances. One client of mine used this *mental blueprint* technique to improve his golf game dramatically without arduous hours of practice, while a shy young woman used it to become a more dynamic and assertive conversationalist and rev up her social life (after having been painfully shy for years). In seven easy steps, you can use the mental blueprint technique not only to master new skills speedily, but to take on the winning ways you admire most.

Breakthrough Technique #3—"Multichannel Thinking"

Ever wonder why some people can solve problems in a snap or come up with creative ideas almost instantly? Chances are they've mastered the technique of using all their thinking "channels" and not just the one or two that most people get by with. Now with the easy multichannel thinking exercises in my book you can actually prime your mind to think more creatively, solve problems, learn and apply new information quickly. And, as an added bonus you'll discover how multichannel thinkers use their skill to get along better with different types of people.

Breakthrough Technique #4—"The Mental Pentagon"

By using your "mental pentagon" you can now direct your own personal "war" against illness and, along with your doctor's treatment, help yourself get well more quickly. Based on recent scientific research on the power of positive thinking in healing disease—even cancer—this technique often works where using only conventional medicine fails. For instance, one of my clients conquered a raging ear infection by using her "mental pentagon." Another highly stressed businessman used it to ease the symptoms of his irritable colon. And, just a few minutes a day spent on the mental pentagon technique can actually help promote health and vitality and *prevent* illness.

Breakthrough Technique #5—"The Inner Power Generator"

At the root of every habit you've tried to break is a particular kind of inner conflict—*not* lack of motivation or willpower. Now with the "inner power generator" system you can substitute desirable behavior for unwanted habits; it's the technique I used to stop smoking; it's what a doctor friend used to stop his pattern of destructive drinking at parties and what one young woman used to turn a lifelong habit of overeating into new-found confidence and health promoting lifestyle.

Breakthrough Technique #6—"The New Hypnosis"

If you can read the writing on this page, you have the innate ability to hypnotize yourself. At the end of my book I'll reveal several methods for what I term "the new hypnosis." Through self-hypnosis you can make every technique in my book even more potent. With the safe and easy induction methods I describe, you can hypnotize yourself to erase unreasonable fears, ease minor pains and aches from illness, increase your powers of concentration and reinforce the new skills you've mastered with this guide!

The real beauty of using *Triggers* is that the improvements, which you choose to make, are *programmed* into your personality. That is, once installed, these changes work automatically. You hardly have to think about it. For instance, you might program yourself with high powered motivation to get a better job. Then, whenever the chance presents itself, you will find yourself eagerly hustling for interviews, getting advanced training, or doing whatever needs to be done to get that better offer.

With *Triggers*, you can program every fiber of your nervous system to make the changes you need to achieve success in all aspects of your life.

Contents

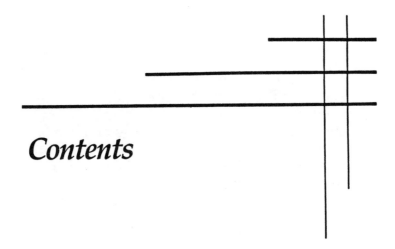

1

How To Motivate Yourself To Do Anything *with* Triggers

Motivation is an inner idea or emotion that prompts you to take action. It is a vital ingredient of success: To achieve your goals, you must work actively toward achieving them. Many excellent plans have foundered on the rocks called "I'll do it tomorrow." You may have fine goals and a creative plan to achieve them, but unless you actively pursue them, your dreams will die stillborn. You have to work your plan. You have to get out and do it.

People who are not motivated to do what is needed are losers. A loser keeps putting off what needs to be done. As a student, a loser doesn't do his homework and then prays he is not asked questions in class. When called upon to perform, he may try to throw up a smoke screen by talking about irrelevant topics, or he may simply retreat in embarrassment.

As an executive, a loser has reached the limit of what her present company can offer and fails to look for another company with more opportunities. She remains unfulfilled, with many of her skills wasted.

This happened to one of my clients who worked for a small family-owned advertising firm. She designed many successful ad-

vertising campaigns that markedly improved the company's financial position. Furthermore, she made some reorganization suggestions that heightened the firm's efficiency and made the company
more competitive. However, as brilliant as she was, she never could
become head of the company—that position was reserved for the
owner's two sons.

She languished at this dead-end job for years, lacking the motivation to make herself either change companies or start her own
business.

A talented artist friend has promised to paint a landscape for an
influential woman who could further his career. He has started paint-
ing the landscape, but only works on it in bits and pieces. He may
never get it done. He dreams of becoming a successful artist, but his
talent is wasted for lack of sufficient motivation.

The dreams of dreamers can lead to great achievements. It has
been said that the world is divided between dreamers and doers, but
this is not true. The world is divided between dreamers who only
dream and dreamers who also *do*. All great people are dreamers—
and more. They actively pursue their dreams, and most of them enjoy
the pursuit. Not only do they put in the time and effort, but in spite of
frustration and disappointment, they continue in their pursuit. They
know how to motivate themselves.

How many times have you had something you wanted to do but
couldn't get yourself to do it? How many times have you started to do
only a little piece of a project every once in a while, but never finished
it? How many times have you let a good idea go to waste because you
lacked the motivation to put it into effect? How many times have you
seen somebody else succeed using the same idea that you had?

Simply wanting to do something, even if your desire is strong, is
not always enough to cause you to act. Many people wish to do things
but never act on their wishes. The world's newsrooms are filled with
reporters who would be authors, but they never write a novel. Many
workers in unsatisfying jobs never finish the education or training
they need to move on to better positions. Many lonely people never
get around to meeting with friends. Any many people, dangerously
out of condition, never start an exercise program.

Such people often are accused of not wanting what they say
they want. Yet I have seen too many people who display an intense
desire to pursue their goals and yet fail to do so because they cannot
put their will into action.

This chapter shows you how to program your mind to turn on, at your command, the essential requirement for success— motivation. You will learn how to make and use *triggers,* a simple, powerful mental technique. Then, by using a system called *double triggering,* you can convert mere desire into action by tapping into your own natural resources. This will enable you to act on your dreams, to do things you have never done or finish things that, up until now, you have kept starting but never finished. You will be able to do things you never thought possible.

Not only can you make yourself do what you need to do, you can really enjoy doing it. No longer will you need to push yourself with "I really should," or wish it were all over. Instead, you will eagerly welcome the opportunity to do it—whatever "it" is, whatever "it" takes.

Using triggers, you will be able to motivate yourself toward your dreams. Life will become a great joy. And you will be able to inspire others to help you in the pursuit of your goals.

THE SECRET OF MOTIVATING YOURSELF

After a hard game of racquet ball I often will sit with my partner, breathing hard, dripping wet, thoroughly exhausted. Our favorite joke is, "If somebody paid me to work this hard, I'd quit." Yet, there we are, paying for the privilege. Between games, I enjoy recalling exciting plays, such as smashing by partner's return ball so low to the floor that he can't reach it in time. I will eagerly look forward to the next game and enjoy buying a new racket or a pair of shoes occasionally.

I realized that it is how you feel about an activity that counts— whether you label it in your mind as work or play, obligation or privilege, misery or fun.

I wanted to write a book, but I did not feel as eager about writing as I did about racquet ball. I could write in a beautifully paneled study with a large window overlooking a splendidly wooded area. My chair was comfortable and, to add to my pleasure, a stereo surrounded me with appealing music to delight my ears. Yet with all this comfort and all my desire, I had never written an article for publication, much less a book. My problem was getting myself to take the time and effort to do the writing.

I tried everything I knew to get myself to write. Simple willpower did not work. Behavior modification techniques were a little better, but too boring to keep me writing. I did do some writing, but it soon became a struggle again. I began making excuses and kept putting it off, finding other things to do that I enjoyed more. The underlying problem was still there. I did not enjoy writing enough to be eager about it, so I gave up in four days.

It wasn't until years later, when I learned about trigger techniques and their amazing power to help people change, that I finally was able to motivate myself to do anything I wanted.

HOW I USED TRIGGERS TO MOTIVATE MYSELF TO WRITE

Now I'm going to tell you about this method to motivate yourself that really does work.

First, decide what outcome you want. I wanted to write, and I decided that I could do this if I enjoyed writing more than almost anything else.

Second, think of something you already enjoy doing. For me, that was fishing.

Having decided the desired outcome and chosen something I already am highly motivated to do, I imagined myself writing, looking at the paper, seeing my hand and the pen, hearing the faint scratch as I wrote and feeling the sensations inside me. As I was thinking about this intensely, I pushed down on my left knee. This created a "trigger," a one-trial conditioned reflex that would call forth these same sensations whenever I pressed my knee in the same way again.

Then, I imagined myself fishing—except when I was feeling that joy I feel when fishing, I pressed the other knee. I now had two triggers. The next step was for me to fire off these triggers at the same time by pressing both knees. This is called *double triggering* and produces both sensations simultaneously. After some momentary confusion, the two opposing feelings merged. Finally, I mentally rehearsed writing. I imagined myself writing in various places with this new eagerness I had just created for myself. I also imagined myself as a successful author reaping the satisfactions and rewards of this achievement.

It was done. From that time on, I was a writing fool. The joy of fishing had erased the old reluctance to write, just as an old song on a tape is recorded over, or erased, by a new one. The entire procedure had taken less than twenty minutes.

Anything you want to do can be affected by this method, which erases a negative feeling and replaces it with a positive one. You must, however, be sure that the positive feeling is stronger than the negative one.

These positive feelings are in your memories of past experiences. They are called your *reservoir*. One of the positive feelings in my reservoir was fishing. The behavior you want to change in yourself is called the *target*. My target was writing.

HOW TRIGGERS TAP YOUR HIDDEN POWERS

A *trigger* is anything that brings forth a memory or emotional feeling. There are five kinds of triggers — visual, auditory, sensory, gustatory, and olfactory. Marriage albums, for example, are visual triggers that awaken those special memories of that event. Couples with a special song have an auditory trigger that arouses emotions and evokes all the other senses in that set of memories, causing the lovers to recall the sounds, sights, smells, tastes, and feelings of special times and places.

Another example of an auditory trigger is the old joke about the comedians' convention. Everyone there knew all of the jokes by number. So all the master of ceremonies had to do was call out "number twenty-one," and he got a laugh. If he called out "forty-two," he got another laugh. The numbers were triggers for the actual jokes.

Triggers can be established easily. You can use any sound, sight, or even a touch. You could also use an odor or flavor, but these generally are too cumbersome to use for our purposes.

To use a sensory trigger, first recall a memory from your reservoir. When the memory is clear enough for you to see, hear, and feel in your mind, you merely have to apply pressure to any part of yourself. You can press a knee, squeeze a thumb, make a fist, bring your hand to your forehead, or blink your eyes. Whenever you want to awaken those same memories, you only need to touch yourself again, in the same way, and those memories will come back instantly. This is called "firing your trigger."

You can use sound as a trigger by tapping a table, saying a word, or producing a tone. Make the sound when the memory is clear. You have created a trigger and only have to repeat the sound to evoke the memory.

You can also use visual triggers, such as looking at your watch or some other object. For our purposes, touch is probably the simplest trigger. You may recognize what I have been describing as Pavlovian stimulus-response conditioning. An astonishing discovery is that humans can achieve this on the first pairing of stimulus and response. This is called "one-trial learning." However, some psychological experts believe that more than conditioning is occurring at these times.

Nevertheless, once created, a trigger can be fired whenever needed to recreate its effect. When my enthusiasm for writing wanes, I just press my right knee in that same way and I am enjoying my writing again. If I want to feel high and excited in some situation (such as an important meeting), I merely press my right wrist, which is a trigger I have associated with the thrill I felt the first time I got up on water skis. This asset from my reservoir erases any mild fatigue, reluctance, or other blocks that might be in my way.

HOW TO BUILD A POWERFUL RESERVOIR
OF POSITIVE FEELINGS

If, in your estimation, you do not have a single memory in your reservoir that is more powerful than the negative feelings you are trying to erase, you can build one by combining a series of memories. For that matter, you can use fantasies. A memory is only a fantasy that has been defined as real.

Recall a series of memories that contain the positive experiences you need. As each one becomes clear in your mind, touch yourself in exactly the same way each time. This will build up your trigger. When you touch yourself that way again, all those memories will activate at once, with a cumulative effect. You will then have a powerful trigger with which to transform your target.

HOW TO MAKE MENTAL REHEARSAL WORK FOR YOU

The last step in the double-triggering system, you will recall, is to practice mentally. Imagine yourself performing your target behavior with your new feelings.

This is done for two reasons. First, scientific studies prove that practicing something in your imagination can be surprisingly helpful for improving skills. Second, imagining your target this way tests whether the procedure has worked. If you can enjoy yourself experiencing the target behavior in your imagination, and the image feels realistic, you can do it in real life. If you can't imagine yourself doing it, or the image is not believable, it is extremely unlikely that you will be able to do it in real life.

It is essential that this image of your new target behavior looks, sounds, and feels real or believable to you. For instance, when I used triggers to make myself write, I imagined myself writing on my boat. But I knew I would never write when I had a chance to be boating. If I couldn't be fishing, I would be preparing my fishing tackle, or talking to someone about the best fishing spots. So I adjusted the image to mentally practice writing in places that felt real to me, such as in my office or my study, and it worked extremely well. Be sure to adjust your last step this way. Also, be sure to frequently see, hear, and feel yourself reaping the rewards of achieving your target.

Here is an outline of the steps to use to increase your motivation to do some activity. Although you could use sound or sight as your trigger, this is an example of how to achieve the desired result by using your sense of touch.

EIGHT STEPS TO INCREASE YOUR MOTIVATION

1. Decide what your target and reservoir will be.
2. Imagine your reservoir vividly (fishing, dancing, reading, or whatever you most enjoy). Create a trigger by pressing your right knee.
3. Imagine your target, and, when it is clear in your mind, create another trigger by pressing your left knee.

4. Using your intuition, be sure your reservoir is definitely stronger than your target.
5. If necessary, build your reservoir's trigger until it is stronger.
6. Fire off both triggers at the same time by pressing both knees, remembering both your reservoir and your target.
7. Allow a minute or two for this to combine.
8. Imagine yourself in the future, performing your target with your newly acquired eagerness. Adjust this image so it feels real. Imagine the *rewards* of performing your target successfully.

You can use this outline to make notes to yourself, which you might want to refer to while you are doing the procedure.

I also used this technique on what, for me, is a tougher problem than getting myself to write—cleaning "the room." We have a large, rambling house with one large room that used to be a two-and-a-half car garage. It now serves as a storage area. I had a bad habit of putting things there "temporarily" until they were piled all over the place in utter chaos. It was frustrating when I wanted to find something in there, but when I faced the prospect of cleaning it up, I felt my stomach twist and I became unaccountably tired. After a few minutes of feeble attempts, I found something "more important" to do.

So, I went through this double-triggering routine, which helped. Now I can enjoy working on the room and straightening it up for only about an hour. The reason this outcome was not outstanding was because my abhorrence of cleaning that room almost equalled my enjoyment of fishing. As I said before, the trick is to pair the undesirable feeling with a much stronger, enjoyable one.

PSYCHOLOGICAL "MONEY IN THE BANK": YOUR VAST RESERVOIR OF HIDDEN POWERS

You can transform your life by using this system to motivate yourself. Inside you is a vast reservoir of strengths and abilities you can draw on. When I use the term *reservoir,* I am speaking of those internal human resources such as enjoyment, trust, caring, enthusiasm, and courage. Infants are born with the motivation to get all their needs met—to suckle, to be held, and to be cuddled. You know how strong these drives are when you see a baby contentedly nursing or cooing as it is being held, and how strenuously it screams if this is withdrawn. Eric Berne, author of *Games People Play*, talks about our inborn "stimulus hunger," a general desire to have our senses stimulated. Later, nature adds the motivation for sexual pleasure to our drives.

As you continue to grow, you channel these drives into pursuing many gratifications. As a child, you may have played in a sandbox, made roads and tunnels to run your toy cars on, tenderly rocked your doll, flown your kite high in a bright blue sky as you felt the string tug in your hand, walked through the woods while marveling at nature, or read about faraway lands where people have fascinating customs.

Childhood joys are potent. When you were a child at play, you were not only enjoying the moment, but also creating valuable habit patterns and learning how to enjoy life in general—valuable additions to your reservoir.

Further resources come from experiences when you were determined, persistent, courageous, or confident. These experiences are part of you and, just like "money in the bank," are the reservoir you can draw on to transform yourself. Having such qualities in your reservoir is what is meant by such statements as having "character," "grit" or "the right stuff." They are there for you and you can make a trigger for any of these qualities. It does not matter how far back you have to go to recall them. What's more, you can even use imaginary experiences as resources for qualities you need.

HOW TRIGGERING HAS HELPED OTHERS

Here are some real life examples, taken from my professional practice, of how this system has been used with different targets being transformed by various inner resources.

At my Clinical Training Seminar at the Veterans Administration Medical Center, I have taught some of the professional staff these techniques to help others change. They were all graduates of accredited schools and trained psychotherapists.

During one session, as part of their training, four students worked with each other to increase their motivation, using the same methods I have been describing to you, except they were applying them to each other instead of to themselves. Having explained the procedure to the class, I asked them to think of something they would like to do more often.

"I'll lead the first one as a model for the class," I said, "and then you will pair up and work on each other. Now, who will begin?"

"I have something," said Rachael. "I used to play the piano a lot, but since I had my baby, I haven't been practicing as much as I want to. She's four months old now and I tell myself to practice, but I never seem to get around to it anymore. I used to really enjoy it."

"Okay, Rachael. Make yourself comfortable and we'll take care of that for you."

Turning to the class, I explained, "Her target is to play the piano more frequently. Now, we need something from her reservoir. What do you really enjoy doing, Rachael? Something you look forward to and do almost every chance you get?"

She thought a moment before her face lit up with a big smile. "Playing with my baby," she said. "She's so much fun." Rachael was easy to work with because she had an expressive face that revealed when she was thinking of her reservoir. However, I was not certain I could read her face to know precisely when she was imagining this, so we arranged for her to signal me when she was.

"Playing with your baby will be your reservoir," I said. "Relax and imagine yourself playing with her. See, hear, and feel that." When her face lit up again, she signaled she was into her fantasy as I had instructed. So I pressed her right knee, creating a trigger for that response. "Now, just as vividly as you can, imagine yourself playing the piano. Give me the signal when you have it."

"Now compare your reservoir," I said (as I pressed her right knee), "to your target" (as I pressed her left knee). "If your reservoir is stronger, give me the signal."

She immediately signaled that it was.

"Good. Now, imagine them together," I said, as I pressed both knees at once.

She frowned, looking puzzled. This is a common reaction when the two sets of experiences are merging. When her face appeared calm again, I knew she had combined her target with her reservoir. This transformed her target, giving her a new mental set about piano playing.

At this point, I told her, "Think of yourself in the near future playing the piano with your newly acquired eagerness." Again, a big smile lit her face as she signaled that she was doing as I had instructed. But the signal was not necessary. I could tell by her expression what was going on inside her. I gave her a few minutes to complete this phase.

Her eyes fluttered open and she excitedly told us that she had also figured out how to find the time to practice. This was a bonus benefit for Rachael. However, it is not necessary to do this during this procedure because, once you create the desire, you will find the time on your own.

Another student, John, voiced a concern he had: "Might you not switch the two feelings, so that you'll dislike what you used to like and like what you didn't like before?"

"A switch wouldn't occur," I answered. "What you are doing is mixing and combining the two sets of experiences—the target and the reservoir—so that the stronger influences the weaker. However, it is possible to make both experiences unenjoyable. So it is important that the reservoir experience is stronger—the stronger, the better."

"You mean if the reluctance is stronger than the drive that's in the other experience—if the negative is stronger than the positive—then you might end up not caring to do either one of them?" John asked.

"Yes, theoretically that is right," I replied. "Although I never heard of it happening."

The next person to try double triggering during that training session was Russ. He was willing to reveal his target to us, but—for the sake of demonstrating that this method works on any target (unless you have a phobia about it)—Rachael, after checking with him that an irrational fear was not stopping him, did double triggering with him without any of us knowing his target.

This way of working can be useful to protect privacy in groups where people know each other and a client is embarrassed or shy about letting others know his or her problem. Instead of saying what it is, he can merely state in general terms the change he wants. This avoids the possibility that others might change their opinion of him and treat him differently. He does not have to worry about what others might think of his personal problem.

Since we knew that Russ wanted to do more of something, Rachael went through the same procedures with Russ that I had gone through with her, but she had to talk in generalities instead of being specific.

At the next session, he reported that the double triggering had worked splendidly. He had been feeling "lazy" about going to his karate lessons, but since his double triggering session, he had attended enthusiastically. As his reservoir, he had used reading. "I jump into a book any chance I get," he said.

At a later class, Russ used an advanced trigger technique (described in Chapter 7) to get over his Vietnam combat nightmares, which had been plaguing him almost nightly for years.

HOW A TARDY WORKER USED TRIGGERS TO CHANGE A THREATENED DEMOTION INTO A PROMOTION

Besides using triggers with students, I use them with my clients.

One man, who worked for a major automobile company, was getting in serious trouble because he was always tardy in submitting his reports. His boss had been lenient with him for years because my client was such a skillful engineer that it made up for his late reporting. In the past, both he and his boss had put paperwork low on their "must-do" list.

Later, Washington put tremendous pressure on the automotive industry to reduce pollution in exhaust emissions. The boss needed reports promptly so he could coordinate work with other departments. However, my client still delayed writing the needed reports. He was even threatened with a demotion and a cut in pay. What used to be a fun job was fast becoming a hassle.

We used the double-triggering technique to solve his problem. When he came to see me, he confided, "I just can't get the feeling that writing reports is the real work. It's just a game." When I asked him what he enjoyed doing the most, he told me that he played bridge every chance he got. He had even been in games that lasted all night. This was used as his reservoir, and writing reports was his target. Triggers were made for each one. Then he checked to be sure his positive trigger was stronger. Next, he double-triggered, transforming his distaste for writing reports into the interest and enthusiasm he felt when playing bridge.

Later, he happily told me that his job had become fun again. He churned out a steady stream of reports about his crucial work on reducing auto pollutants. His boss was delighted with the change in his work. Instead of being threatened with a demotion, my client was given a promotion and was awarded a nice fat bonus.

HOW TRIGGERS WERE USED TO REVITALIZE A DEAD-END CAREER

An executive in the dead-end advertising job also use double triggering to advance herself. The resource she used from her reservoir was her love for her young son. This woman would go to any lengths to care for her little boy. For instance, she searched for just the right nursery school for him, gladly spending the hours and energy needed to make a thorough research of the available schools.

When it came to her job, her target was to look for a better career opportunity. She used the double-triggering technique and began to feel almost as eager about taking care of herself as she did about taking care of her son. With the use of triggers, she landed a job with good promise, and with her natural talents, she easily won recognition and soon had a position worthy of her talent.

HOW A LONE WOLF USED TRIGGERS TO BECOME A SUCCESSFUL ORGANIZATION MAN

Another interesting example is the case of the owner of a large business. He was a lone wolf who used triggers to make himself a successful organization man.

Having invented a specialized tool that came into great demand, he started his own business. Singlehandedly, he built it into a large successful company. He spent hours alone at his desk going over figures and making detailed plans about his business. He enjoyed running his business this way, and this enjoyment helped make him such a successful businessman.

However, his company had gotten so large that he had to hire managers and delegate responsibility. This meant that he had to make a change in his business style. He had to meet frequently with his managers to give them his advice and guidance so they could benefit from his superior business judgment. The trouble was, although he wanted to do it, he did not enjoy meetings and did not attend them as he knew he should.

Nor did he want to reduce the size of his business to the one-man show it had been, because it would cost him an important competitive advantage.

When we talked over the problem, it boiled down to the fact that he wanted to keep his large organization intact and he wanted to enjoy his work as he used to.

"If only I could enjoy meeting with my managers the way I enjoy working alone in my study. I'd be all set," he said.

It was a simple matter to make a positive trigger for working in his study, and then another target trigger for meeting with his managers. His positive trigger was easily stronger, and when he double triggered, his feelings about meetings were transformed. He could easily imagine himself enjoying working with his people.

When he went back to work, he found himself having a good time working in this new efficient way. He always welcomed an opportunity to share ideas and work out solutions. His managers were also delighted that the "boss" became so accessible to them.

HOW OTHERS HAVE MOTIVATED THEMSELVES WITH TRIGGERS

Here are some other examples of how the triggering technique was used to help people reach their goals. One woman, who desperately wanted a divorce, needed to brush up on her typing skills so she could support herself. She disliked typing, so I had her double-trigger typing and her love of needlework. This transformed her feeling about typing so she not only did the needed practice, she also was surprised at how much she enjoyed typing and her job. She gained enough financial independence to start a new life for herself as a free woman.

Another nine-year-old girl I was seeing in family therapy was getting excellent grades in mathematics, but disliked social studies and was barely passing. When I asked her if she would like to enjoy social studies, she wrinkled up her nose and rolled her eyes for a while before agreeing she would. I combined her feelings about mathematics (which she "loved") with those about social studies. Then I had her picture herself learning social studies in the future. She now gets above average grades in social studies, while still maintaining excellent grades in mathematics.

There are countless applications for this surprisingly simple but powerful system. So practice this technique to motivate yourself to do something you want to do but feel some reluctance to go ahead with or just can't seem to find the time for.

MAKING TRIGGERS WORK FOR YOU

If you are having trouble making the triggering method work for you, there are several possible reasons.

1. Begin with an Easy Target

One problem might be that you started by trying to change too difficult a target. Begin with something easy until you gain more skill and success. This approach is used when attaining most new skills. After all, you wouldn't try to learn to drive a car on a busy downtown street. Instead you would choose a quiet residential street or a lonely country road.

Start out with something you already like to do, but would like to do even more. Write this target down on paper, along with other targets. Number your targets in order of increasing difficulty, putting those you like to do first and those you dislike last. Then, you can start transforming your motivation with those items on the top of your list and work your way down.

A person who likes to visit friends but just doesn't get around to it, does not care too much about exercise, and dislikes job hunting would have a list that looks like this:

1. Visit friends more often
2. Do my exercises
3. Look for a better job

Work on only one of your targets at a time to give yourself enough time to adjust and practice the change in real life.

2. *Use Strong Reservoirs*

The second reason that double triggering may not be working for you could be because the positive experience from your reservoir was too weak. Remember, it has to be stronger and more vivid than your target. Check this out by imagining both the target and the reservoir, so you can compare the two in your mind. The assets that you take from your reservoir should contain strong feelings of fun and desire, something you can see yourself doing or something that sounds good to you. Things that you now spend much time doing are excellent assets to use. If you do not have one experience that contains enough of these assets, you can build one up by combining two or more until they create a strong resource, as described earlier on page 6.

3. *Use Three or More Channels*

The two preceding corrective measures should clear up most difficulties. However, another problem could be that you are not able to imagine vividly. Some people have an underdeveloped imagination. Ideally, you should be able to see, hear, feel, smell, and taste mentally what you imagine. The first three senses are the main ones that we use in our culture. If you cannot at least clearly see, hear, and feel in your imagination, these and other mind-expanding techniques will not work well. Fortunately, you can develop this skill, as explained in Chapter 4. After you become adept at doing mental exercises, you will be able to successfully apply these motivation techniques.

4. *Mentally Rehearse*

Remember the last step, mental rehearsal. Imagine yourself enjoying your target behavior in the future, so that it feels believable to you. Change the image until it feels right to you. Include images of enjoying the rewards of performing your target behavior.

5. *The Special Case of Phobias*

A somewhat different situation exists if you have been trying to motivate yourself to do something toward which you have a phobic reaction. Phobias are irrational fears about some object, animal, or situation. The fear is irrational because it is out of proportion to the actual threat. Even if it makes sense to be a little fearful of an object or situation, the phobic person's response is exaggerated. To tell if your target is a phobia, ask yourself if the reason you are avoiding the target is because you are afraid. Phobias are dealt with in Chapter 2.

6. Stopping Yourself from Doing Something Requires a Different Method

If you are trying to motivate yourself *not* to do something (smoking, overeating, etc.), you will have to use a different method to change your behavior. This is because such targets often fill hidden psychological needs. Appropriate methods for dealing with this are discussed in Chapter 11.

A troubleshooting checklist follows that summarizes what to do if the method is not working for you. The list will help you decide how to correct your techniques so you can get the results you want. Go through this list and find the particular problem you are having with the techniques. When you identify your problem, read the solutions in the right-hand column and apply them.

Troubleshooting Chart If Double Triggering Does Not Work

Possible problem	Solutions
1. Target too difficult	Choose an easy one, work up to harder ones
2. Reservoir experience weak	Find a stronger one. Build two or more
3. Mental rehearsal is not realistic	Adjust it until it feels believable
4. Target is a phobia	Read Chapter 2
5. Imagination too weak	Read Chapter 4
6. Trying *not* to do something	Read Chapter 11

You will find that this double-triggering method is far superior to ordinary willpower.

More sophisticated variations of the double-triggering technique are explained in Chapter 2, and additional applications of it will be described throughout the book. This will enable you to use triggers to improve many other areas of your life.

2

Triggers for Erasing Unreasonable Fears

Everyone has fears. The most powerful of our emotions, fear can save your life by stopping you from dashing across a busy street without looking or from sticking your hand in a hungry tiger's cage. If we didn't have fear urging us to flee from danger, we would have vanished as a species long ago.

In contrast to helpful fears, irrational fears handicap you in the pursuit of your goals. A student who avoids asking questions of his teacher is clearly hampered in his ability to learn. Similarly, a businessman who avoids talking to bankers or a boss who has trouble saying "no" to her workers is handicapped. One excellent salesman wasted countless hours during which he could have been selling, because he was afraid to fly.

PHOBIAS: UNDERSTANDING THE ENEMY

An irrational fear is a phobia, an unfounded fear of something, causing the victim to avoid a certain dreaded object or situation.

Phobias are more widespread than you may imagine, especially when you consider the social phobias. These are irrational fears that involve other people: fear of speaking in public, examination anxiety, shyness, and so on. Phobias can be as mild as stuttering when introducing someone or so severe as to force the sufferer to be housebound.

WHY OVERCOME YOUR IRRATIONAL FEARS?

Irrational fears cause the victim to avoid even positive situations. I am reminded of the case of Marge, an airline executive. One of her job perks was the chance to fly throughout most of the world for as little as twenty dollars. Although she was not afraid of flying, she had a phobia of being in a place from which she could not easily escape—such as the back seat of a car, the middle seat in a theater, or the cabin of an airliner. Due to her unreasonable fear, she had to pass up opportunities to fly cheaply.

From my years of clinical experience, I am convinced that phobias are the primary obstacle stopping so many of us from leading the satisfying lives we could live.

If you have a phobia, it does not have to cause you severe anxiety in order to interfere with your life. Even a persistent, mild phobia can raise havoc in your life. If you have an irrational fear of something that is important to your success—talking to important people, for example—you will become nervous and anxious when you try to do it. If you forge ahead in spite of the anxiety, you pay with discomfort and stress. Your body wants to retreat as you force it forward. Repeated unwanted stress has been linked to countless diseases: ulcers, headaches, heart attacks, and even cancer are only a few stress-related diseases.

More than likely, you will do as most people—you will avoid the object of your phobia. However, doing so will make it most difficult, if not impossible, to reach your goals.

Such phobias may be causing you to make compromises and settling for second best. How many times have your plans been undermined by irrational fear? Are fears, both big and little, running and ruining your life?

THE OLD STRUGGLE TO GET RID OF IRRATIONAL FEARS

Over the centuries, various methods have been used to help people overcome their fears. Two of the oldest methods involve exposing the phobic person to the object of his or her fears — either in small doses or in one massive confrontation. I call the first method the "sweaty palm" method; the other I refer to as the "make 'em or break 'em" method. Both methods rely on the body's adaptation to being overstimulated. If someone is sufficiently frightened without any bad consequences, the fear will wear itself out, and the once feared object will no longer trigger the fear.

The second method, "make 'em or break 'em," does just what it says: either it works, or the victim truly becomes a victim, more frightened than ever. Taking a person who is terrified of swimming and throwing him into deep water either forces the person to learn to swim or will cause an even worse panic.

The "make 'em or break 'em" method is a poor choice because it can make the victim worse instead of better — who will benefit and who will be harmed is unpredictable. On the other hand, the "sweaty palm" method — gradually exposing the fearful person to his feared object in small doses (creating only enough fear to cause the person to sweat) — usually works well. One serious drawback to the "sweaty palm" method is that not everyone will tolerate it.

Since phobias are the cause of so much human misery, therapists have long been interested in this phenomenon. Psychoanalysis, treating patients twice a week for several years, has had relatively few successes. However, modern therapies, which encourage patients to abreact their traumas, get excellent results.

An abreaction is an emotional reliving of the initial traumatic event that started the phobia. The flashbacks experienced by veterans of severe combat experiences are spontaneous abreactions.

In a therapeutic situation, the patient is helped to imagine that the trauma is happening in the present. Like a flashback, the trauma is relived in full intensity (sometimes with the help of phenobarbital or hypnosis). This is similar to the "make 'em or break 'em" idea, except the patient is not thrown into a real situation.

In Vivo *Methods*

Science has reinvented the "sweaty palm" method.

The University of Michigan Anxiety Clinic specializes in curing phobias of all types with the "sweaty palm" method. Of course, such a dignified institution cannot call it that. They call it the *in vivo* method, which means "in life," as opposed to symbolic or imaginary experience.

There are excellent videotapes of live sessions during which the head of that clinic, Dr. George Curtis, cures patients of their phobias. He has shown me one tape of his skillful work with a young woman who was terrified of spiders.

Determined to rid herself of her fear, she allowed herself to be exposed to the object of her phobia — live spiders — which had been carefully selected by the university zoologists and were non-poisonous.

At first, she only had to watch the spiders in a covered glass jar. Next she watched them in an uncovered jar. Then, the spiders were set free on a nearby table. By the end of the fourth session, she was able to feel reasonably comfortable while allowing a spider to crawl up her cheek. As unenjoyable as the experience had been for her, she had gained the satisfaction of attaining freedom from her phobia.

I was especially interested in watching Dr. Curtis' work. I was comparing it with the cures I had achieved using triggering procedures. I had just recently learned them, and I found these methods a lot easier and faster than fooling around with live spiders. It was also simpler than the abreactive methods I had been previously using.

Furthermore, abreactive and *in vivo* methods are difficult procedures for people to endure. Although the experience of facing one's fears is seldom as bad as anticipated, not all people are willing to do this. Some never try, others drop out of such programs.

In most cases, these difficult procedures are no longer necessary. You don't have to suffer to get better. Double-triggering methods can erase unreasonable fears easily, comfortably, and rapidly.

THE BENEFITS OF ELIMINATING YOUR FEARS

Some phobias don't create much of a problem. For example, if you are a city dweller who fears snakes, you can easily avoid them. However, those phobias that cannot be avoided, cause you undue anxiety, or interfere with reaching your goals are significant and should be mastered. Being free of significant irrational fears will benefit you greatly. The chronic anxiety created by a phobia causes depression. Eliminating the phobia eliminates this anxiety and cures the depression. And, more importantly, the road to reaching your desires will be smoother. You will be in charge of your life, making your life more gratifying.

I often hear my clients describe how their lives have improved since they have erased their phobias and are no longer ruled by their irrational fears.

For instance, one of my clients was a brilliant man, but his career was being sabotaged by a groundless fear. Whenever the boss was present, he clutched up and kept his ideas to himself. He knew that if he only could speak up and explain his ideas to his boss, he would be on his way to the top. Time after time he watched his coworkers suggest ideas that often were not as good as his own. Yet his fear of being criticized by the boss was so great that he could not risk presenting his own ideas — even after seeing someone else get praise for presenting an idea that was similar to his own. Logical arguments that his fear was exaggerated did not help. He already knew that his fear was irrational. However, by using triggers he quickly erased the basis of his fear. Later, he told me, "After using triggers, talking to the boss became easier and easier. I began giving excellent suggestions and my whole career took off like a rocket."

Another client was so in awe of doctors that he never questioned their decisions. For years, he endured painful injections of arthritis medication — although there was a perfectly good pill that would have done the same job. However, he was phobic about questioning his doctor's judgment. It took only one session of trigger techniques to replace his fear with confidence. "What a relief," he later confided to me. "I really hated those injections. Not only did I persuade my doctor to give me pills, I can now ask him questions about my health. It feels good to be able to talk to him man-to-man."

A female client was so fearful of judges and lawyers that she kept postponing getting out of a hopeless marriage, which was making her life miserable. Her husband and she simply did not get along any more, and nothing they did made the situation any better. Her social life was dead — as a married woman, she didn't feel right about dating. She waited for her husband to divorce her, but he never would. Trapped by her unreasonable fear of the legal profession, she felt that life was going nowhere for her. Finally, with the help of trigger techniques, she eliminated her anxiety and talked to her lawyer. "Going through the divorce wasn't too bad. I feel a great weight has been lifted from my chest," she told me later. "Oh, by the way, I just met the most wonderful man."

TRIGGERS DON'T CONQUER YOUR UNREASONABLE FEARS – THEY ERASE THEM

When I first used the trigger techniques to relieve my patients of phobias, it was difficult for me to believe that such fears could be erased so easily. What makes erasing fears with this method easy is not that the process is done entirely in your imagination. After all, imaginative experiences such as nightmares or abreactions can be painful.

However, double triggering avoids all the pain, yet it's extremely effective. You don't *conquer* your fears—you erase them.

Furthermore, the procedure does not require an outside operator. You can do it by yourself. I used to direct my patients through the steps, doing as much for them as I could. I would even press down on their knees to install their triggers. Then I started experimenting with turning over the process to my patients and found they could do the procedures themselves.

HOW MIKE USED TRIGGERS TO GET RID OF HIS FEAR OF APPROACHING STRANGERS

When Mike started seeing me, he was depressed over his inability to work. It took a few sessions for Mike to reveal what was really bothering him. In a sense, he had a phobia about having a phobia. Most phobics are embarrassed about their phobias—and maybe not unreasonably so. They believe that if their problem were revealed they would be subjected to ridicule by friends and acquaintances, or be secretly considered inadequate and regarded with less esteem.

At our early sessions, Mike was able to admit only that he was depressed. A salesman all of his adult life, he could no longer make himself go to work. I was puzzled. He acted and sounded like a competent adult with appropriate responses. He had an easy, relaxed manner and an attractive smile under a distinguishing mustache. He had handsome, masculine features, an athletic build, and spoke in a smooth baritone. His verbal abilities were excellent, and he could argue logically and persuasively.

However he had not worked since he had quit his job a year earlier, and his new wife had recently lost hers. They were far behind in all of their bills. Finally, when he learned that his ex-wife was suing him for back child support, he revealed his fears. He was so ashamed of having an illogical fear, that it took all that pressure to make him admit his true problem.

"I'm scared of going to strangers to try to sell them something," he finally confessed. Once Mike was face to face with a client, he was fine, he said. He presented his wares competently and usually walked away with an order. But he was terrified of approaching strangers, including prospective employers.

Up until then, he had told me that his problem was simply lack of motivation, so we had used the trigger techniques described in Chapter 1. His target was to enjoy selling so he would find a job and do it. He was an avid golfer, and we used that for his reservoir. He seemed to respond well to the procedure during our session in the office. However, nothing changed for him in the real world. Two weeks later, he was still not looking for work. Then, when he explained his fears, I understood why.

Since his problem was not simply a lack of motivation, we had to modify our double-triggering techniques to rid him of his phobia.

Although his target was the same and we could use the same asset from his reservoir, we now needed to know two additional things: the last three times he experienced his phobia, and the first time he had experienced it.

"Tell me the last time you felt frightened about approaching a new prospect, Mike."

"That was the day I quit my job at Simpson's. I had just gotten back from leading a sales seminar. I walked into my office, looked at the phone, and thought about all those calls I had to make to new prospects. I just didn't want to face that anxiety anymore, so I dictated my resignation letter on the spot."

"Let's call that time 'Simpson's,'" I suggested. "Now, recall the time before that when you felt that same kind of fear. Then tell me a short title we can give it just for identification. I don't have to hear the details."

"I guess that would be when I worked for the Anderson Company."

"All right, 'The Anderson Company.' What would be a time before then when you felt your phobia so we can put it next on your list? Just give me a title."

We continued until we had labels for two other memories he had when he felt this irrational fear: "The High School Paper" and "Meeting Jenny's Father." (Jenny was his first wife.)

"Now, tell me when was the first time you felt this fear," I continued.

Mike thought for a while before his eyes widened and he replied, "I never fully realized it before, but that's the same feeling I'd get when I was a kid standing before the door of my father's study. I'd want to ask him for something, but I didn't know what kind of mood he'd be in. He was a minister and could be mean and humiliating to me at times. I never knew when to expect it."

"Let's call that 'Father's Door,'" I said. "Okay, starting from the most recent and going back to your earliest memory of your phobic reactions, we have these: 'Simpson's,' 'The Anderson Company,' 'Meeting Jenny's Father,' 'The High School Paper,' and 'Father's Door.' These are all part of your target. They are called 'subtargets.'"

I had him jot down these subtargets on a card. At the top of the card, I had written "TARGET" in large letters.

"Now, compare that fear you felt with how good it feels to golf. Which is stronger?"

"I can't say it's golf," he said, laughing.

"We need to build up your reservoir so it is stronger. Search through your store of memories and remember a time when you had the kind of feelings you want to have when approaching a strange prospect."

After a bit of thought, he replied, "You know, when I was dating Susan, my present wife, I just felt totally accepted, as if I could do no wrong. I just seemed to know automatically the right thing to say and do."

"Sounds good. When you combine the two reservoirs, 'Golfing' and 'Dating Susan,' do they feel stronger than your phobia?"

"I'm not really sure."

"You can check that out a little later, Mike," I said.

On a separate card, I had him write "RESERVOIR" at the top.

Below this word, I had him write, "Golfing" and "Dating Susan." He placed this card on his lap, along with the one listing his targets.

I began to talk him through the system.

"Think about the first item in your reservoir—golfing. In your imagination, see, hear, and feel it. Smell the fresh air. When it's clear in your mind, press down on your right knee."

When he had done this, I continued. "Now, think of your other reservoir. See it in Technicolor and hear it in stereophonic sound. Include any smell and tastes. When you have it, press down on your right knee again in the same way." This combined both assets from his reservoir, giving him one powerful trigger that would evoke both experiences at the same time.

"Now, think of the last time you experienced your target," I said. He hesitated. "If you can't remember, open your eyes to look at your card."

Mike glanced at it, read "Simpson's," and closed his eyes again to concentrate more intensely.

"When you have this target clear in your mind, make a trigger for it by pressing down on your left knee," I instructed.

Now that he had triggers for his reservoir and target, I told him, "Fire off your reservoir trigger by pressing your right knee. Relive those times (pause). Now, fire off your target trigger by pressing your left knee (pause). Compare the two. Which is stronger? If it's your reservoir, nod your head to let me know what's happening."

He nodded. "That's fine," I said. "We can continue and transform each of the subtargets. Press both knees at once." This action evoked his experiences from his reservoir (golfing and dating Susan) and his subtarget (working for his last employer, Simpson). These experiences mixed through his mind, creating a feeling of confusion. When this subsided after a minute or two, he nodded to indicate to me that the first transformation had taken place.

"Now, think of your second subtarget, the Anderson Company," I instructed. "When you have it in mind, press down on your left knee (pause). Now, press your right and left knees at the same time." This combined his reservoir experiences with the fearful ones he had at the Anderson Company. Again, he held his trigger by continuing to press both knees until the confusion was cleared up. This meant the subtarget had been transformed. It was decontaminated of unreasonable fear, just as the first subtarget had been.

We continued in the same way with the remaining subtargets

until, finally, Mike relived that fearful experience he had had as a boy, standing in front of "Father's Door." As he did so, he created a trigger for it by pressing his left knee. He then fired off the trigger on his right knee to combine that experience with those he had when "golfing" and "dating Susan." This completed the double-triggering. process. Now the original trauma, which had conditioned him to be phobic about approaching strange prospects, was neutralized. The final step was for Mike to rehearse mentally the changes he had just made.

"Now imagine yourself approaching strange prospects with your newly transformed feelings. See, hear, and feel yourself doing it in the future. If you need to, you can press your right knee to trigger those positive feelings." I watched carefully, but he didn't fire his trigger.

"That worked fine," he reported.

Then I suggested, "Imagine asking for a job."

He did so and then commented, "That was interesting."

"Were you able to do it?"

"Yes, it's fairly easy to do. But I sure felt funny earlier when I was imagining all those things at once."

"That's when you were transforming your subtargets by double triggering. That's a common reaction. How did you feel when you imagined yourself selling to a stranger and asking for a job?"

"Those were okay — no problem. But will I feel confident like that when I do it for real?"

"That's the whole idea. The next step is to test it out in the field — the sooner, the better."

"All right, I'll line up a job interview as soon as I can."

"Fine. Call me if it conflicts with our appointment. Otherwise, I'll see you same time next week."

Two days later, Mike called to cancel. He had gotten a new job and would be in training for two weeks. Four weeks later, I saw him and he was amazed at how much easier it was to approach strangers. He was enthusiastic about his ability to succeed.

A year later, I got a letter from him expressing his satisfaction with our work. He had become one of the best salesmen in his company. He had gained such a good reputation that other companies were making him lucrative offers trying to lure him away from his present job. His new problem was trying to decide which offer to take.

FAST AND EASY TRIGGERS TO REPLACE FEARS
WITH CONFIDENCE

If you suffer from an unreasonable fear, you can erase the fear and replace it with confidence. Instead of letting fear control you, you can be in charge and master your life.

This method is an improved version of a method called "Systematic Desensitization" developed by Drs. Joseph Wolpe and Arnold A. Lazarus, authors of *Behavior Therapy Techniques.*

The improved version is called the "Fast and Easy Triggers" method. It uses double triggering and powerful reservoirs, and combines these techniques with Systematic Desensitization. As a result, this new system works more quickly. It usually takes only one session. Also, compared to *in vivo* or abreaction methods, it is much easier on the patient. Clinics that use the Fast and Easy Method report an 85 percent cure rate for phobias.

By erasing your nagging fears that interfere with the way you run your life, you can rid yourself of the primary reason people do not use all of their potential.

Here is an outline of this technique for you to follow. You can place it in your lap to refer to, the same as you can refer to reservoir and target notes. In these examples, I describe creating your triggers by pressing your knees. Of course, you can press any part of your body to create a trigger. Some people prefer to press their thumb and forefinger together to make a trigger, for example. I have found that visual or auditory triggers are less convenient to use.

NINE STEPS FOR THE FAST AND EASY TRIGGERS
METHOD FOR ERASING YOUR FEARS

1. Prepare your cards. Label one "Reservoir." On it, list two or three experiences that have the positive feelings you want. These are your assets.
2. On another card, list five incidents during which you suffered the fear, starting with the most recent incident and going back in time until you end with the first phobic reaction you can remember. These are your subtargets.
3. Create a trigger for an asset from your reservoir by pressing your right knee.

4. Create another trigger for your first subtarget by pressing your left knee.
5. Compare your asset to your subtarget. If the asset is stronger, go to number 6. If it is not, build up your trigger with the rest of your reservoir. (If it is still not stronger, do not continue. Alternatives will be explained later in the book.)
6. Double-trigger by pressing both knees at the same time to evoke your reservoir and your first subtarget together.
7. Create a trigger for your second subtarget. Double trigger your reservoir with your second subtarget. Wait until you feel settled.
8. Continue this with all of your subtargets.
9. See and hear yourself performing your target with the new feelings you have just acquired from your reservoir.

This entire procedure takes twenty to forty-five minutes from the time you start step 1 until you complete step 9.

You should test out your work by facing your phobia as soon as you can. When doing this, if you become worried or begin to feel some anxiety, you can also activate your positive strengths from your reservoir. When you are about to face your feared object or situation (your target), you can press your right knee, or whatever you did for your positive trigger, in the same way you did during your session. This will evoke your reservoir to help erase the fear. However, this is seldom needed.

HOW PAUL AND BEVERLY USED FAST AND EASY TRIGGERS TO SAVE THEIR MARRIAGE

Here is how this Fast and Easy Triggers method was used to save a failing marriage which was being undermined by the husband's unreasonable fear. They saw it as a "communication problem."

"We have a communication problem," said Beverly, who sat with her husband across from me. Her husband, Paul, shot her a sideways glance before agreeing with her.

I thought to myself how frequently couples complain of poor communication and I wondered what was interfering with their talking to one another.

As I watched Paul and Beverly interact, I noticed how Paul always glanced at his wife before saying anything. He also became silent and avoided eye contact with his wife at certain points in the conversation.

At one of these points, Beverly said, "This is what I mean. He clams up and I don't know what he's thinking. Sometimes, he'll hardly talk to me for hours. How can we get anything settled that way?" She burst into tears and Paul looked guilty.

"Gee, I'm sorry, honey," be began.

"Sorry? What good is being sorry?" she shot back. "We've got to talk." She went on, energetically explaining why it was important for her to know what his thoughts were and what he wanted in their marriage. She furrowed her forehead deeply and spoke intensely. Paul gave her that furtive glance and tensed up. He did not answer.

The session continued this way. At the end, little was accomplished, as Paul became more silent and Beverly more angry.

At the next session, I saw Paul alone. He was articulate and spoke easily — not at all like he was when I saw him with Beverly. He admitted that he avoided talking to Beverly at times.

"It's just that I can't figure out how to talk to her about some things without making her mad," Paul said.

"What's wrong with making her angry? When people disagree over things that are important to them, they get angry. It's a way of showing that they really care," I explained.

"Maybe so," Paul said, "but I really feel anxious when she gets mad. In fact, I feel nervous around any woman who is mad. I guess it's because my mother was always flying off the handle. I never was sure when she would be in a bad mood. Sometimes she slapped my face hard. Boy, I hated that. What made it worse was never knowing when she would get mad like that."

"Paul," I asked, "can you see how it would be useful for you to be able to talk to your wife even if she gets angry? I mean, if you could have a choice about it. If you could see that the argument was going somewhere useful, you could continue. If the argument was getting destructive, out of hand, or getting no where, you could *choose* to stop. The way you are now, you have no choice. You automatically clam up."

"I've thought about it a lot and I know you're right. But I get so anxious, I just want to get away. I guess I'm just afraid," he said with embarrassment.

"How would you like to erase that fear you have of angry women?"

"That would be great. But how do I do that? I have been this way all my life," Paul asked.

"Think of the kind of feeling you would like to have instead— the opposite of being scared: confident, in charge, maybe even enjoying yourself. Tell me about a time you had those kinds of feelings."

The assets he used were the good feelings he had playing football—the rougher the game, the more elated he felt. He also listed on his card, under "Assets," a certain look Beverly gives him. "It's like that song, 'When First I Saw the Love Light in Your Eyes,'" he said, visibly flushed and warming to the task.

For step two—list five incidents when you experienced your target (fearing angry women)—Paul listed these subtargets:

Beverly being angry at him last week

Their first argument two years ago

A woman supervisor at work who got angry over his work

A nun at the parochial school he attended

His mother

(You will notice, so far we are merely getting ready to do the real work in the rest of the procedure.)

For steps three and four, Paul created a trigger for playing football. Using multichannel imagery, he imagined the sights, sounds, and feelings of playing football. He created a trigger for this asset by clenching his right fist. Then he made a trigger for last week's argument with his wife by clenching his left hand. He now had his positive and negative triggers.

Next, he did step five and fired first his right trigger. This evoked a vivid memory of playing football. Paul noted the positive feelings in this image. Then he fired his left trigger which recalled the memory of last week's argument with Beverly. Paul noted the negative feelings in this image. When he compared the relative strength of the triggers to each other, he found the feelings in the left trigger stronger, and he had to build up the weaker positive trigger.

To do this, he made a vivid, multichannel image of Beverly's loving look and clenched his right fist again. This combined his good feelings when playing football with his good feelings about Beverly at those times she looked lovingly at him. When he compared the two triggers after building up his right trigger this way, his positive trigger was decidedly stronger than the negative one.

At step six, Paul clenched both fists to fire both triggers at once, creating the usual sense of confusion as the sights, sounds, and feelings of all three of those memories (football, loving wife, and angry wife) swirling in his mind. He waited until the confusion cleared and his feelings integrated.

He went on and created a trigger for the female supervisor—his second subtarget—by clenching his left fist, and then, just as he did before, double triggered until this set of images was integrated. He went on to double trigger the rest of his subtargets: the memory about the nun and the memory about his mother. This completed steps seven and eight.

For the last step, using multichannel imagery as always, he imagined himself with his newly transformed good feelings when dealing with angry women. He imagined arguing with Beverly and carrying the argument to a successful conclusion.

I also had him imagine an argument with her that he decided to stop for a while because it was going nowhere.

Now he had choices about how to react to angry women. He no longer had to retreat from them. Instead of being controlled by his phobia, he was in control of himself. He would be able to handle confrontations, with his wife and other women, the way he thought best.

At the next session, Paul was a changed man. He looked Beverly straight in the eye when they disagreed. Both reported they were beginning to get things straightened out between them. Although some of their arguments were painful, they were able to start settling important issues. Beverly was pleased, but she admitted that it was difficult for her to get used to not automatically having her own way.

At a follow-up session three months later, they both reported their relationship was much better. The threat of divorce was gone and they felt secure. In fact, they were planning on having a child.

You can apply this double-triggering technique to an endless list of irrational fears. My patients have used it to overcome a host of fears including fear of closed-in places, flying, swimming, crowds, public speaking, school examinations, physicians, sex, standing up for themselves, and asking for dates.

ANOTHER WAY TO STOP FEAR FROM RUNNING AND RUINING YOUR LIFE

Sometimes the irrational fear is so great, that your reservoir is not strong enough to submerge it. When you compare the strength of your reservoir to your target, the assets in your reservoir sometimes do not feel stronger than your target. Nor can you build it up enough to be stronger. In that case, do not use the Fast and Easy techniques. Instead, use another system, which I will describe below. It is designed to handle such problems.

As I suggested earlier, transforming targets with reservoirs is based upon the pioneering work of Wolpe and Lazarus. At a time when conventional therapies, such as psychoanalysis, were having disappointing results with phobias, these doctors achieved cure rates better than 85 percent. They erased one emotion with another, as does double triggering.

Their method uses relaxation exclusively as the reservoir. The doctors deeply relaxed their patients and paired this relaxation with the target, which they called a symptom. Obviously, relaxation is a desirable response as opposed to irrational fear. But relaxation is a weak reservoir, compared to fear. The got around this problem by using a different system for designing subtargets.

One way of getting over a fear is to overcome it in small stages. For example, if you want to rid yourself of a fear of swimming, you might start by just spending some time on the beach. Then, you might stand or sit at the water's edge for a while. Later, you could go into very shallow water, and then eventually work yourself into the deep water. Drs. Wolpe and Lazarus used this principle in designing subtargets for desensitizing phobias.

I use a similar system, which I call the Slow and Easy Triggers method, for erasing phobias. This method combines powerful triggering techniques with the techniques used in systematic desensitization. This makes for an exceptionally effective method.

HOW CECILIA OVERCAME HER FEAR OF DRIVING

I resorted to the slower method with a patient I'll call Cecilia. After having been in a serious automobile accident, Cecilia was afraid to drive her car more than three or four blocks. She came to me for help, but, even with building one asset on top of another, we were unsuccessful in finding assets in her reservoir that were powerful enough to transform her fear.

She lived a considerable distance away and was understandably disappointed that the Fast and Easy method wouldn't work for her. It would be inconvenient for her to stay in town for the six to fifteen sessions that the Slow and Easy system would take. I suggested that I could teach it to her and she could go home and do it herself. She eagerly agreed.

First, she wrote on separate cards all of the situations in which she was afraid to drive, including those in which she felt only the slightest anxiety, plus those in which she felt absolute panic. Because relaxation is a weak reservoir, it's important, in this procedure, to have at least one subtarget that evokes very little anxiety. She rated each subtarget on a scale of one to ten, one being the least frightening.

The cards were then arranged in numerical order — the weakest first. The strongest was placed last and the others put in between. They were ranked according to how much anxiety they caused her.

For example, when Cecilia only made plans to drive her car, she felt the least anxiety. When she rode in a car with someone else driving, she felt more anxious than just sitting in a parked car. However, when she drove the car a city block herself, she felt still more anxious, and so on. So, these situations were ranked on her list, as shown below.

Cecilia's Ranking of Her Subtargets

1. Planning to drive the car a short distance.
2. Getting into the car and sitting in it.
3. Riding in a car.
4. Driving a car one block.
5. Driving four blocks.
6. Driving one mile.
7. Driving three miles.
8. Driving five miles.
9. Driving on an expressway (the accident had occurred on an expressway) a few miles.
10. Driving a long distance on an expressway.

A person's subtarget list is highly individual. Someone else with a similar irrational fear of driving would rank similar items in different order, as well as have different items that frighten her. For example, I treated a man who found that the most terrifying situation for him was riding in a car with someone else doing the driving.

Cecilia took her list and her instructions with her. To erase her irrational fear of driving, she was to apply the Slow and Easy Triggers method at home. Although riding home with her husband was an ordeal, she could manage it.

When I saw her some time later, she proudly boasted she had driven all the way from Algonac, a town over 200 miles away in northern Michigan, herself. "I used your techniques on myself and it worked beautifully. I can drive whenever I want, wherever I want. It's great. I used to feel so dependent on other people, it was like being trapped. You don't know what it means to me to be able to drive myself. Now I'm free," she said.

Naturally, I was pleased with her success, and I was curious about how well she followed my instructions. As she described how she did it, I saw that she followed them precisely.

When she returned home, she went to her room and put her subtarget list in her lap, concentrating and imagining a scene that was personally soothing and peaceful for her. She liked the woods in the fall when they are ablaze with color and the air is cool and smells fresh. This image gave her three channels: the sight of the trees, the smell of the air, and feeling of the temperature. She made a trigger for this reservoir by pressing down on her right thigh.

Next, she imagined her first subtarget, sitting in her living room making plans to drive her car a short distance. She made a trigger for it by pressing down on her left thigh. The anxiety in this scene felt weaker to her than the good feelings about being in the fall woods. Her positive trigger was stronger than her negative trigger, so she could proceed.

Cecilia double-triggered, pressing down on both thighs at once, so that the images of the fall woods and planning to drive her car were recalled at the same time. The two images merged. Her reservoir transformed this first subtarget. Then she fired her positive trigger only, and just enjoyed an imaginary walk in the woods. This is called "taking a vacation."

To ensure that the subtarget is completely transformed, she

repeated this a few times. When she felt certain that transformation had taken place thoroughly, she went on to her next subtarget and double triggered her image of the woods with her image of walking to her car. Again, after allowing the images to integrate, she fired only her positive trigger. She repeated this procedure a few times: double trigger, integration, then single trigger.

Cecilia proceeded in this way with each item on her list. She had to double trigger the last four items seven times before she was desensitized. It was a slow process, taking her many hours, which she broke up into fourteen sessions.

After each session, she practiced *in vivo* the steps to which she had desensitized herself, but absolutely went no further. If she had imagined herself comfortably driving only one block, she would actually drive the car one block and no more.

At the end of four weeks and fourteen sessions, she had completed the procedure, gotten in her car and driven down the expressway, free of her unreasonable fear.

The following list outlines the steps she used for curing her irrational fear.

TEN STEPS FOR ERASING IRRATIONAL FEARS

1. Divide your irrational fear into subfears. Arrange these subtargets in order of increasing anxiety.
2. Imagine a scene where you feel comfortable and confident. Create a trigger for this reservoir.
3. Create a trigger for your first (easiest) subtarget.
4. Be sure your reservoir is stronger than this subtarget.
5. Double-trigger your reservoir and subtarget.
6. After they merge in your mind, trigger your reservoir only ("take a vacation").
7. Repeat steps 5 and 6 until you are completely comfortable triggering the subtarget.
8. After step 7, you may end the session. Do not confront any subtargets that you have not mastered yet.
9. Make a trigger for your second subtarget and repeat steps 5, 6, and 7.
10. Continue the procedure with each of your subtargets.

When you can comfortably imagine yourself doing the most feared activity comfortably, you have succeeded. You have automatically performed the concluding step of trigger methods: imagining yourself doing the desired activity.

In-between sessions, before you have completed the entire process, you may confront a sub-fear (sub-target) to which you have already desensitized yourself. Do *not* confront any fears to which you have not yet desensitized yourself.

A POLITICIAN OVERCOMES HIS FEAR OF PUBLIC SPEAKING

One of my patients was an ambitious politician who was afraid of public speaking. He used the Slow and Easy Triggers method to free himself of this conflict.

He was quick-witted, verbal, dedicated to sound government, and could inspire followers during informal conversations in small groups of two or three. Of course, to succeed at politics, he had to be able to speak to large audiences. However, when he forced himself to do this, he felt terribly anxious. It was so painful for him that he was about to give up his political career.

He was not able to build up a positive trigger that was stronger than his anxiety, so he started a course in the Slow and Easy Triggers method. For his positive trigger, he used the confident feeling that he enjoyed when discussing his ideas with his best friend. He divided his target into nine subtargets:

1. Speaking to three people
2. Speaking to four people
3. Speaking to five people
4. Speaking to eight people
5. Speaking to twelve people
6. Speaking to twenty people
7. Speaking to forty people
8. Speaking to a hundred people
9. Speaking to a large audience

He did well on his desensitizing program. After each session, he would limit the number of people he talked to, depending on how far he had reprogrammed himself on his list of subtargets. When he ended a session where he felt confident imagining himself talking to eight people, he arranged to talk to groups of only eight or less. These meetings went well for him. For the first time in his life, he enjoyed addressing groups.

At his next triggering session, he felt good imagining talking to twelve and then twenty people. Afterwards, he arranged to speak to a group of about fifteen people at a nearby community college. Unfortunately, about forty people showed up since he was becoming popular as a speaker, and he clutched up and was just as scared as ever. He managed to make a respectable presentation, but it was difficult for him.

He felt discouraged and almost gave up. I convinced him that the trigger techniques would still work, and he continued with the Slow and Easy Triggers system. He had to start at the beginning of his subtargets again. However, he was careful not to expose himself to too large an audience before he was ready. This time, he completed the entire program and was able to enjoy speaking to large audiences.

He became known as a composed and witty speaker, which allowed him to realize his full potential and successfully pursue the career he desired.

Even more ironic than a politician afraid of public speaking are the many cases I have treated of people who yearn for love, yet who are afraid of the opposite sex. Many people lead unhappy, restricted lives because of such problems.

Almost all phobias will respond to the Slow and Easy Triggers method if the Fast and Easy method, which Mike and Paul used, doesn't work. Obviously, these procedures can eliminate much unnecessary misery and sweep away obstacles to achieve your personal goals successfully.

3

Breakthrough Trigger Techniques To Improve Your Learning Ability Dramatically

Living in the age of "the information explosion" makes it imperative that we learn and retain new information as rapidly as we can.

Taking care of your health, selecting a mortgage, buying (or deciding not to buy) a computer, making intelligent political decisions, understanding the latest art and literature demand that you digest an enormous amount of new information if you are going to get the most out of modern living and not be left behind.

For example, in the financial area, the income tax laws are altered every year. Some years, the changes amount to a major overhaul. Understanding the intricate new changes can save you thousands of dollars. Buying a new car presents you with a complex variety of choices, but to take advantage of this choice requires learning a mass of new information. Financial institutions are offering better ways to save and invest your money, but it is up to you to choose the right one for your particular circumstances. Again, there is a lot to learn.

Similarly, in the arts, more material than ever before is being produced by an army of creative talent. You are presented with a dazzling variety of works. Choosing which ones merit your limited time means more information to assimilate.

Although basic wisdom and common sense remain most valuable, we need to keep well informed in order to be able to speak effectively and engage in well-rounded conversations. With the proliferation of different lifestyles and changing values, staying up-to-date can be especially helpful for parents. It improves their ability to communicate with their children and other young people.

There are small, but no less important, social benefits from being able to learn and recall certain details. We tend to be impressed and delighted with people who remember our favorite activities, interests, and other personal information about us: our favorite music, the names of our children, or the nickname by which we like to be called.

We also respect someone who can back up her opnions with background information about her position. Facts, along with enthusiasm, are persuasive.

For many of us, our jobs are constantly being upgraded with new information. Younger people enter our field with updated knowledge, and new technologies are regularly introduced. Therefore, we have to learn constantly, just to stay even—getting ahead requires even more effort.

Fortunately, there is a triggering technique that you can use to learn and recall new information. It hones your learning ability to a fine edge and allows you to learn at your peak ability whenever you want to, allowing you to master material quickly and efficiently.

THE LEARNING TRIGGER SYSTEM FOR MASTERING NEW INFORMATION

Learning is not complete unless you can recall information when you need it. So, in a practical sense, learning is a two-phase process: acquisition and retrieval—putting the information in our memory system and getting it out. To achieve this, a single trigger— the *Learning Trigger*— is constructed, using the following principles.

The Scientific Foundation for the Learning Trigger System

Psychological research has shown that learning is often situation-specific. You will best remember what you have learned when you are in the same place you learned it. In one experiment, a group of students was divided into two groups. Both groups studied in the school gymnasium and each student was given the same material to learn in a given period of time.

At the end of the study period, each group was separated. One group stayed in the gymnasium, while the other was taken to a regular classroom. Then both groups were given the same test on the material they had studied. Those who took their test in the gymnasium (the same room they had studied in) did significantly better than those who took the test in a different room, demonstrating that the closer you recreate the same conditions under which you learned the material, the better you will be able to recall it.

The learning trigger will mentally transport you to the situation you were in when you learned your information. Just as the subjects who stayed in the gymnasium remembered more when tested, you also will remember more.

A similar principle pertains when police use hypnosis to help a witness recall details that he does not remember during routine questioning. Under hypnosis, the witness imagines himself at the scene and in the emotional state he was in at the time. If he was frightened at the time, being in that same mood will bring back the memory of those events that frightened him. Then a witness often can remember important details.

Since recreating the mood you were in when you learned something helps you remember it, you could study your material when frightened or angry and then recreate this mood with a trigger. However, it would obviously be unpleasant to do it this way.

Instead, you can create a pleasant study mood for yourself and build this mood into your learning trigger. Then, whenever you fire it, it will recreate this same emotional state within you. Then, if you need to recall your information when you happen to be in an emotionally charged atmosphere and feeling anxious, this trigger will recapture your pleasant study mood and dilute your anxiety. Besides being more enjoyable for you, you will be seen by others as calm and, therefore, confident.

HOW MAX USED THE LEARNING TRIGGER SYSTEM TO OPEN THE DOOR TO A REWARDING CAREER

Max wanted to pursue a career in hotel management. He was emotionally honest, highly personable, tactfully persistent, and loved to travel. This would make him a valuable employee for the hotel chain for which he wanted to work.

Yet his ambitions were being frustrated because he had trouble concentrating and absorbing new information. He needed to finish college and get his degree. His problem with learning was preventing him from reaching his goal. He was bright, once he learned his material. However, when trying to study, he was easily distracted and could always find something else to do that was more fun than studying.

Furthermore, Max often became anxious when he was questioned about important information. He would balk when his professor asked him a question. During these times, it was difficult for him to remember the answer. He wondered how he would respond to questions from a future boss or important customer.

To help Max achieve his goals, we turned him into an excellent learner by using the Learning Trigger system. He was instructed to recall from his reservoir those times when he was attentive and enjoyably absorbed in something. For Max, it was those times he stalked deer. An avid hunter, he focused his full attention and concentration when doing this.

Using the techniques explained in Chapter 1, Max made hunting a positive trigger: when he could see, hear, and feel himself (in his imagination) stalking a deer, he created a trigger for it by placing his chin in his hand, as people often do when thinking. Since this looks natural, Max could fire his trigger in public without arousing attention from others.

Next, by pressing his left knee, he made a trigger for the reluctance he felt about studing. (An advantage to making a trigger at a spot that is not handy to reach is that you are not apt to fire it accidentally.)

He compared his two triggers and found that the positive one was stronger. It was safe to double trigger and he did so, transforming the feelings he had about studying.

Now, whenever Max fired this trigger, it put him in an especially attentive mood and enabled him to concentrate just as intensely as he did when hunting. He was able to concentrate on his studies and focus his full attention. Max became almost as avid about studying as he was about hunting. This automatically enabled him to learn more.

This is part of the magic about triggers: It helps you study more often. Triggers cannot show you how to get something for nothing. To learn, you have to study. However, in addition to helping you study more often and have fun doing it, the learning trigger will help you learn more effectively.

The rest of the steps in the system build this one learning trigger into a multiuse trigger than will activate additional learning skills.

To build the next learning skill into his learning trigger, Max was instructed to place his hand on his chin to activate his trigger before each study session. In addition to creating the efficient study attitude described earlier, this conditioned his trigger so that firing it in the future, would help him recall his material easily and swiftly.

Now, whenever he needed to remember what he had studied, he could fire his trigger. Although it was impractical for him to go back to his study desk when questioned, the trigger would take him back there in his mind, mentally reactivating his study situation and putting him in the same mood he was in when he learned the material. In the same way that the students who remained in the gymnasium remembered more, Max remembered more.

Multichannel Thinking: The Secret of Turning Your Imagination into a Powerful Teaching "Machine"

Max also was able to further improve his ability to recall material by using another powerful technique based on the pioneering work of men such as Noam Chomski, Karl Pribran, and Wilder Penfield. Chomski, author of *Language and Mind,* is famous in scientific circles for his work in linguistics. Karl Pribran, author of *Languages of the Brain,* is also famous for this work with imagery. Penfield is well known for his experiments, while he was director of the Montreal Neurological Institute, eliciting vivid recall in patients by electrically stimulating the cerebral cortex.

From the work of such pioneers has evolved a model of mental functioning that is an important guide for telling us how to expand our thinking abilities. The majority, perhaps all, of our thinking and remembering involves using our five senses.

Most of us can picture an object in our mind — for example, you can remember a friend's face by visualizing it well enough to recognize her in a crowd. You match the real face you see with your eyes with the one you see in your head. However, you may not be able to see the mental picture well enough to remember which one of your friend's eyes is slightly larger (most people's eyes are of a different size). Can you imagine what a saxophone sounds like and see in your mind's eye a silver one and a brass one? Imagine what it feels like to make a snowball with your bare hands, what a rose smells like, what sugar tastes like. The ability to sound the words in your head as you read, or hold mental conversations with yourself are additional important skills.

Some of you, who do these things easily, may be surprised to learn that some people have difficulty thinking with all five of their senses. I know a well-educated woman who cannot visualize. If you ask her to picture her own children in her mind, she reports that she cannot. However, she can recognize them when she sees them, as well as recognize her friends and acquaintances. However, she gets lost easily, failing to recognize landmarks with which she should be familiar. When driving, she constantly has to read street signs or count how many blocks she has traveled.

On the other hand, her hearing ability is well developed. She can remember lectures and conversations well. She also is sensitive to the tone of voice people use, and is good at understanding the hidden meanings behind the words that they say. However, if she had better visual abilities, she would be more competent and life would be easier for her.

These mental pictures, sounds (including words), feelings, smells, and tastes have been called "mental facsimiles," "representational systems," "ideo-depictions," "covert behaviors," and "cognitions" by theorists. For brevity's sake, I'll refer to them as "channels." We have a channel for every sense, but because we use them so automatically and rapidly we seldom are aware of how we do it. This is just as well, because such an awareness would only slow us up. However, understanding them is useful for our present work.

The more senses you can consciously represent in your imagination, the better. The techniques based on imagery will work more powerfully, you can be a better hypnotic subject, artistic talents will be more well developed, and both intuitive and intellectual learning will be greatly aided. In addition, multichannel thinking probably has other advantages that we do not even realize.

Chapter 4 will tell how to increase your ability to use your various channels. The Learning Trigger System relies heavily on multichannel thinking and assumes that the reader can already use at least three channels. If you cannot, you can use the mind-building exercises that are given in Chapter 4 to develop powerful multichannel thinking.

When it comes to using multichannel thinking for learning, research suggests that the best students in our educational system are good at using the seeing and hearing channels. These are efficient channels with which to recall information. So powerful is the visual channel that many students use only this one. (Of course, hardly any of these students are schooled in consciously using their channels. Most just do so unconsciously.)

For instance, when it comes to spelling English words, see-ers have it all over those who, instead, use their hearing channel to sound out the word inside their head. This is because English words are not always spelled as they sound. Visualizers will see the word *knife* in their imagination and know to use the silent k, for example.

By using your seeing channel instead of your hearing one, you can improve your spelling. Get in the habit of looking at words and, when they are spelled correctly, generate a pleasant sensation inside you. If you have trouble generating such a sensation, borrow one from your reservoir. Think of something that makes you feel good and, at the same time, look at the word. The word becomes a trigger for that feeling and, whenever a word makes you feel good, you will know it is spelled right.

Do the opposite for misspelled words. When you see them, create an unpleasant feeling by thinking of something like rotten eggs. Then, whenever a word gives you that unpleasant feeling, you will know that it is spelled wrong. Or, if you want to avoid unpleasant feelings, think of something silly and laughable whenever you see a misspelled word. Either way will work, as long as it is clearly different from the feelings you generate for yourself when you see correctly spelled words.

Understanding how successful students use their channels to master material was gained from field studies. Researchers would observe skillful learners in naturally occurring situations and interview them to find out the methods that they used to learn so well.

In addition to field studies, a study under controlled laboratory conditions was recently made to test the effectiveness of multichannel learning. Under the auspices of the U.S. Army Research Institute for Behavioral and Social Sciences, Doctors David Meir and Owen Caskey compared a group of 134 college students, who used several channels to learn their material, to a matched group who studied in their usual way. The study showed that mental imagery is, indeed, a significant aid to learning.

The researchers concluded that there is nothing as powerful, as effective, and as easy to use as the human imagination. Multisensory imagination is the world's finest teaching machine, and we all possess it. We simply need to learn how to use it.

How Max Used His Channels to Master Complex Subjects Easily and Quickly

Since Max was able to use his visual channels well, I instructed him to practice seeing the pages of his books and notes in his mind's eye. Max would activate his study trigger and visualize the material he needed to remember. He would put his hand to his chin and then read the information as it appeared in his mind's eye. Some clients imagine a crystal ball or a TV set and "see" their notes or books in it.

In addition to being able to read his mental notes, he also recalled material in his hearing channel. When he fired his study trigger, he mentally saw and heard a teacher or colleague talking about the desired subject. Max would "hear" his teacher and "see" what was being written on the blackboard.

Emotional involvement is necessary to master learning. Even great chess masters who play such a cerebral game become excited as they play. Bobby Fisher, the American chess champion, would get excited and make loud exclamations.

To engage all channels and to attach a positive emotional tone to his material (dry, dull material is difficult to remember: exciting, fun material sticks in the mind), Max played with his study subjects. He indulged in multichannel fantasies.

For example, for his biology studies, he imagined he was the size of a microbe and taking a fantastic voyage through a human body. He was accompanied by a gorgeous microbe-sized woman clinging to his arm. She "oohed" and "aahed" at his knowledge and expertise about the "terrain."

When studying history, he became each king's special advisor. Max fantasied steering the king through the political intricacies of each ruler's era. Max would not only see and hear these fantasies, he would feel the excitement and gratification of being involved in historic events. Max used fantasies for anything he wanted to learn well.

To complete the Learning Trigger System, Max fired his trigger and practiced testing himself on material that he was studying. He engaged two channels by giving himself both oral and written quizzes. He would either imagine the test or actually use a paper and pen. This gave him the feel of the pen and the movement of his muscles as he wrote, and further engaged his feeling channel.

Now, Max had built his trigger so he was able to store what he wanted to know in several channels, and his trigger was conditioned to recall the tested material in all of these channels. Max had built a powerful learning and recall ability into this one trigger.

"LAYERING" ALLOWS ONE TRIGGER TO TAP ALL YOUR LEARNING ABILITIES

Although we have been building the same trigger as a multiuse trigger to tap different reservoirs and skills—such as motivating yourself, creating a learning attitude, keeping yourself calm, and enhancing recall—your mind will automatically bring the right one to the fore when needed. When you want to absorb something new, firing your learning trigger brings out your intense concentration. Then when you fire your learning trigger to answer questions, another appropriate resource automatically comes forward. Your other reservoirs will be present, but in the background. This process of building different reservoirs into one trigger is called *layering* because reservoirs are built up like layers in a cake.

When the learning trigger is fired, the calm study mood will always be tapped and be the underpinning for whatever else you are doing: learning new material or recalling it. When you are fielding questions on the public firing line, your relevant learning fantasies, crystal balls, written and oral quizzes, sights, sounds, and feelings of your material will flash through your mind so swiftly that they will be practically unconscious. You will be thinking more rapidly and clearly than ever before.

Here is a summary outline of the seven steps for the Learning Trigger System. It assumes you have no examination phobia or similar performance anxiety, or you have removed it with the methods described in Chapter 2.

SEVEN STEPS FOR THE LEARNING TRIGGER SYSTEM

1. Create a trigger for a time you were enjoyably engrossed in some learning activity. Make this trigger stronger than any negative feelings you may have about studying.
2. Fire this learning trigger before each study session.
3. During each study session, fire your trigger and practice visually recalling your material.
4. Similarly, during each study session, fire your trigger and practice recalling your material with your hearing channel.
5. Indulge in fun fantasies about the material you are learning. Use as many channels as you can.
6. Fire your trigger and practice recalling your material with oral and written quizzes.
7. Whenever you need to recall the information studied, fire your trigger.

To recapitulate, the learning trigger is built in layers so that by using one motion, such as holding your chin in your hand, you bring all your learning resources into play. The learning trigger uses the double-triggering principles covered in Chapter 1—it motivates you to study and puts you in a learning frame of mind. In addition, this trigger is associated with your study sessions so that whenever you want to recall something, you mentally put yourself back in the situation where you learned it. As we have learned, this increases your ability to remember.

Also, the learning trigger has you automatically use multisensory learning. This trigger is built to access your seeing, hearing, and feeling channel. The Center for Accelerated Learning, in Lake Geneva, Wisconsin, scientifically proved that multichannel study improves learning and recall.

Further, the learning trigger evokes the mood you were in when you learned the material. Besides making recall better, it enables you to be in that pleasant mood regardless of the circumstances you are in when you need to remember. Max doesn't clutch up anymore when an authority figure asks him questions.

Building all these abilities into one trigger is much more convenient than having several and trying to remember which one to use when. The single learning trigger gives you a convenient, powerful tool for mastering knowledge.

Since using the Learning Trigger System, Max graduated with honors and found a job selling convention space for a large hotel chain. He travels all over the country, staying at the best hotels. Hawaii was especially enjoyable for him. He is building a reputation as the best-informed worker in the entire chain. Not only does he know his job inside and out, he is mastering the data about his bosses' job—all the policies and procedures, the interoffice memos, and the pricing structure. Max is expecting a promotion soon.

With these powerful new techniques, you can dramatically increase your ability to learn, retain, and recall new information and knowledge. Of obvious benefit to students, these techniques are immeasurably useful in most learning situations.

HOW NANCY USED TRIGGERS TO PUT HER CAREER BACK ON TRACK

Even if you are able to concentrate well, there probably are times when you are faced with having to learn a lot in a short time. The Learning Trigger System is extremely helpful in such situations.

For example, Nancy, a young automotive executive, found herself struggling to get her career running smoothly again. She had taken time off from her job to have her baby. Now she was back, and she was faced with learning all that went on in her large, fast-breaking company while she was away.

The automotive industry had been going through many changes. These changes included technological improvements in the cars, as well as changes in the organization and management of Nancy's company. She had to learn a large mass of material. New policies had been made, personnel had been changed—some had been transferred, others promoted, and others had their jobs redesigned so they did things differently and had different responsibilities. As she was learning about these old changes, current information had to be mastered.

At meetings, she needed to contribute her ideas to the discussion and decision-making process. However, she often did not have enough information about some projects.

Furthermore, Nancy felt anxious during meetings because she was the only female executive in the department. Although most of her co-workers judged her on her performance, some males made it clear that they felt her job needed to be done by a man.

To get up-to-date on her job, she had a lot to learn and learn it quickly. However, although she took material home, she found it hard to make herself study. Even though she desperately wanted to carry out her responsibilities, she was exhausted from trying to use her will power to force herself to learn all of the material. She was depressed and had problems sleeping.

Nancy came to me about her problem and I explained that the Learning Trigger System was made-to-order for her situation. She enthusiastically started learning the Seven-Step Learning Trigger System.

As you will recall, the first step is to make a trigger to access a time when you are effectively involved in something that fascinates you. We easily learn about things that we are deeply interested in. Nancy used her fascination with growing flowers—especially hybrid roses—as her resource for making her learning trigger.

Nancy's high motivation to learn about these flowers was transferred to learning about her job. She felt a deep, almost mystic inner peace when working with roses. This feeling would help dilute the tension she felt when she needed to come up with answers at work.

She vividly imagined the sights, sounds, feelings and the smell when working with and learning about roses. This gave her a powerful four-channel image that was much stronger than her reluctance to study material about work.

Instead of holding her chin, as Max had done, she chose to press her thumb and forefinger together to fire her trigger. She preferred not to touch her face. Pressing her thumb and finger together was easy and unobtrusive.

Following the second step of the system, she fired this trigger whenever she needed to learn something new, such as when reading a new directive, listening to an expert present new information, or going over her notes. At meetings, when new material was being presented, she fired her trigger. This put her into a learning attitude and she absorbed the information readily. Sometimes she forgot to fire her trigger and she found her attention waning. She then would fire her trigger and become attentive again.

When building her learning trigger, Nancy would often review in her mind what she was studying. She combined steps three and four, and practiced recalling material with her seeing and hearing channels. Holding her finger and thumb together, Nancy imagined a crystal ball. In it, she saw her written material or saw and heard someone who had explained the information to her earlier.

If the images were not clear enough for her to get the information, she would review her real notes, memos, or books, and then repeat this step until the images were clear enough and gave her the information she wanted. Once or twice was usually enough.

Some of my clients who use the crystal ball technique can read the actual words. But when Nancy visualized her study material in a crystal ball, she could not read it. Nevertheless, she could easily recall the essence of what it said.

Later, upon questioning, Nancy realized that when she "looked" at her material in the ball she heard the words in her mind. This is called *bridging,* an important technique that will be described in the next chapter.

For step five, indulging in fun fantasies about the material to be learned, Nancy fantasied about using the new information with key people in her organization. Fanciful situations, which worked so well for Max, did not appeal to down-to-earth Nancy. However, she was stimulated by imagining herself using her knowledge in realistic situations, such as addressing the weekly staff meeting or suggesting an improvement in procedures to her boss. In these fantasies, she saw and heard the interactions and felt her emotional reactions. For her, the give-and-take of business dealings was exciting fun.

To further ensure reliable recall of material when she needed it,

Nancy used step six. She fired her trigger and wrote summaries of what she had learned.

HOW TO USE TRIGGERS TO PLUG MATERIAL INTO YOUR MEMORY — FOREVER

Nancy made sure to review important material that she wished to retain for a long time. Since memory for new information decays within a short time—between a few hours and a few days—it is important to review soon after learning something. Once something is relearned this way, the memory for it decays much slower, so you need only review it in a month or so. By then, the new material is mastered and you only have to review yearly to keep the information available to you.

So it pays to use your learning trigger and review material you have worked hard to learn. The effort to review is small compared to the original effort you made to learn something. To repeat, a good schedule is to review right after you learn something, then the next day, then the next week, and again the next month. After that, to remember something forever, you only need to review it every year or two. Studies show that much of what we learn is lost if not used within three years.

At work, Nancy used step eight, firing the trigger to access needed information. She pressed together her thumb and finger to recall the material. In high-pressure situations, using her trigger not only recalled the material she needed, it also recreated the enjoyable feelings Nancy felt when working with roses. Her fellow workers were impressed with her poise and she gained a reputation at work for having all the important information "at her fingertips."

In a relatively short time, Nancy had regained the ground she had lost during her absence. She was able to show her competence to her boss, and her career was back on schedule.

HOW A BUSINESS WOMAN USED LEARNING TRIGGERS AND SAVED THOUSANDS OF DOLLARS A YEAR

A business woman used the Learning Trigger System to learn the income tax laws so she could consult intelligently with her accountant. Although he did a respectable job, she knew from direct experience that her employees never put as much effort and concern in her business as she did. She reasoned the same would be true for her hired accountant.

She happened to be a skillful airplane pilot and easily learned anything having to do with flying, so she based her trigger on her interest and love of this activity. She then used the seven steps to build a strong learning trigger.

Soon she was enjoying learning about taxes and suggested to her accountant something he had overlooked—a new way of taking depreciation that legitimately saved her thousands of dollars a year in taxes. Instead of overpaying money to the government, she could now invest it in her business.

With the new infusion of cash, she was able to make her business flourish. Her accountant thought she was something of a wizard to learn so much about taxes in so short a time.

She was delighted with the power of her learning trigger, and used it to learn anything important to her.

HOW A SPORTS ENTHUSIAST USED TRIGGERS TO INCREASE HIS SOCIAL POISE

Another client increased his social poise and became popular by using the Learning Trigger System to improve his memory.

He wanted to feel more comfortable with people and be better liked. But, although he liked people, he had trouble remembering personal things about them—what their interests were, their political positions, what they enjoyed doing, when their birthdays were. He often was embarrassed when he realized he was asking a friend about something he had been told some time earlier.

Scientific research has demonstrated that those who are able to form clear visual images have better social memories. Psychologists William Swann Jr. and Lynn Miller of the University of Texas found that good visualizers are able to remember details about people they have met—their background, values, likes, and dislikes. Therefore, they were significantly less likely to suffer the embarrassment of making social slips.

Although he was a good visualizer, my client did not apply this skill to social situations. Fortunately, he had a powerful resource in his reservoir. He was a sports nut. He could tell you all kinds of details about the subject. Friends called him a walking sports encyclopedia. When he created a trigger with his fascination with sports, he was able to build it into a effective learning trigger for learning details about people he met.

When people were telling him things about themselves, he fired his trigger. Later at home, he would again fire his trigger and review what he had learned. He made up fantasies in which these people were professional athletes, playing in tournaments, honored at banquets, being interviewed on television and so on. Upon seeing these friends and acquaintances again, he only had to fire his trigger to remember all he had learned about them.

In a short time, his friends and acquaintances were noticing how thoughtful he had become. All of a sudden he seemed to be more caring, and people were attracted to him. They did not realize that he seemed more concerned because his memory about them improved.

For his part, he felt more at ease because he no longer was making social blunders by forgetting things. He began to have a lot more fun with people. "I've really increased my social batting average," he commented.

Like everyone who learns the Learning Trigger System, he found a great many things for which to use the system.

There are countless applications for the Learning Trigger System. Using the instructions and examples given here, you can design a personal learning trigger for yourself and use this powerful tool to further your goals and enrich your life.

4

How To Expand Your Creativity Up to Five Times with Multichannel Thinking

Most people are one-channel thinkers and go through life specializing in their favorite mental channel. Some are see-ers, others are hearers, and still others are feelers. For example, to recall the color of one's living-room rug, a visualizer will use her visual channel to "see" an image of the rug in her mind's eye. You might even notice her glance down as she is trying to recall this, just as if she were in her own living room looking at her rug. A hearer will hear in his mind the word for the color, while a feeler will recall the sensation he associates with that rug and that color.

It is with these channels derived from our biological senses that we form most, if not all, of our memories. Although largely an unconscious process, it can readily be brought to awareness by paying attention to how you think.

What has been said about memory also holds true for other forms of thinking — planning, analyzing, and problem solving. We take the impressions embedded in our channels, and selectively manipulate them toward our ends. The see-ers among us will see solutions to problems, hearers will talk them out, and feelers will work them out. The last two channels, smell and taste, are not as frequently used for intellectual learning. Yet research indicates that these channels are useful for intuitive thinking. Some people sniff out solutions, or find which course of action doesn't leave a bad taste in their mouth. These phrases are more than just figures of speech. They are descriptions of how we actually think.

HOW MULTICHANNNEL THINKING
GREATLY EXPANDS CREATIVITY

Since each channel has its special strengths to help us learn and think, the ability to use each of the channels is a valuable skill. As we have seen in the last chapter, multichannel thinking dramatically increases your learning ability. It also opens up new ways of thinking. A good engineer, using two channels, will use memories stored in his visual channel to design the form of a trestle, then use his auditory channel to verbalize the mathematics for figuring how strong each part should be.

The great theoretician Albert Einstein used his channels in a similar manner. He used his visual channel to create "thought experiments." These were experiments conducted entirely in his imagination while rigorously applying the laws of physics, just as if the experiment were being conducted. He would visually imagine what would happen in nature if certain things took place — for example, traveling at the speed of light. Then he would use his verbal channel to compute the mathematics entailed in his "thought experiment."

Dancer Isadora Duncan used her feeling and visual channels to create her art. She would feel the emotions she wanted to convey and then make up new routines that visually expressed to the audience what she felt.

The ability to use different channels can also add new dimensions to your personality. For instance, someone who doesn't use his feeling channel will be insensitive to other's feelings. This can cause problems in getting along with others.

In addition, a multichannel thinker can establish better friendships with a wider range of people. Scientists have discovered that good friends think in the same channel. Feelers will have "heart-to-hear talks," visualizers will "see eye-to-eye," and hearers will "tune in to each other." One-channel thinkers will limit themselves to friends who think in the same channel. However, if you use all channels, you will be able to relate well with most people. Regardless of which channel another person uses, you can match it and communicate well with them. Modern sales teams are learning to use this principle to increase sales. Progressive lawyers and teachers are also using this principle to increase their persuasive powers.

WHY ONE-CHANNEL THINKING BLOCKS YOUR PROGRESS AND LIMITS YOUR LIFE

Unfortunately, many people are blocked from solving certain problems because they use only one channel. Their customary channel is not always the best one for achieving their goals.

Such was the case of a client I'll call Bruce. Like the woman mentioned in the previous chapter who couldn't visualize her own children, Bruce's visual channel was also underdeveloped. He was a feeler and did not do much with other channels. Since he was adept at thinking with his feeling channel, he was acutely keyed into other people's emotional reactions and able to be unusually sensitive and tactful. Besides helping him be a fine husband and father, this responsiveness to interpersonal relationships enabled him to work well with people at his job at a large electronic company's personnel department.

Despite all this, Bruce was an underachiever because he had to learn a lot of new information quickly, similar to the cases of Max and Nancy in the previous chapter. Bruce just could not keep up with all of the new rules and directives that were a necessary part of his job. When dealing with employees, he would sometimes mistakenly operate under outdated policies or overlook a new rule. Once, when arranging to transfer some technicians to another division, he arranged them to have interviews with the wrong executive. Lines of authority had been rewritten, but Bruce hadn't learned this. When the first technician showed up for his interview, there was much confusion and consternation until the error was cleared up.

Due to such problems, Bruce spent too much time undoing mistakes or looking up the rules and regulations. Although adequate workers in his company get routine annual raises, Bruce was afraid that he wasn't going to get his raise.

Bruce needed to absorb efficiently the new information required on his job. To do this, he needed good visual skills because visual channels are much more efficient for that kind of learning. We needed to reactivate and strengthen his underdeveloped visual channel. We did this by drawing on the work of Wilder Penfield, cited earlier.

WHAT "BRIDGING" IS AND HOW IT EXPANDS YOUR MENTAL POWER AND CREATIVITY

Much has already been written about Penfield's work, but one of his findings bears repeating here. When he electrically stimulated the brain's cerebral cortex of a conscious surgical patient, the patient recalled past experiences in all five channels with extreme vividness. Stimulating the area on the brain's surface which controls seeing still evoked a five-channel memory. The same thing happened when Penfield stimulated the brain's auditory and other areas. All channels are connected. Our memories are stored in all five of them.

A more common example of another channel being connected to the favored channel was given in Chapter 3. When Nancy used her visual channel to "see" her notes in an imaginary crystal ball, she was not able to read the notes, but she could "hear" what they said—being able to vaguely see her notes helped her to hear what was written in them. She created a bridge from her visual channel to her auditory channel. Recalling something in one channel will stimulate the other channels embedded in that memory. This is called "bridging" and is a valuable talent that you can teach yourself.

You can achieve this ability by practicing a series of mental exercises that use the bridging technique. These exercises start with your strongest channel and then bring out your weaker channels. By doing these exercises, the weaker channels become stronger and readily available for your use. Then you can approach problems more creatively. A problem whose solution lies hidden from your visual way of thinking may readily be solved when your other channels are brought to bear.

For example, I helped an interior decorator who, as you would expect, had excellent visual abilities. He went into business for himself and became in great demand because of his visual creativity. But his business suffered financially because he was poor at math. Mathematicians are good with their auditory verbal channel, which they use to solve problems. When the interior decorator used bridging exercises to develop his auditory verbal channel, he became much more competent in the financial end of his business.

To give Bruce, our personnel worker, the many advantages of multichannel thinking, we designed the following mental exercises.

HOW BRUCE USED MENTAL BRIDGING EXERCISES TO MASTER HIS JOB AND LAND A RAISE

The first thing Bruce learned was how to use his dormant visual channel. We constructed pleasant imaginary experiences that would begin with his strong channel and bridge to his weaker ones — from feeling to seeing or hearing. (The content of these imaginary experiences should not be unpleasant because the mind's natural defenses against noxious emotions would come into play and interfere with the learning process.)

First, he relaxed, concentrated, and imagined the following scene:

> I feel the warm, humid night air against my skin. As I stroll along a sandy beach, my bare feet sink into the dry, warm sand. Looking down, I see the white sand as my feet step along the beach. The sand keeps getting deeper so that my steps become more difficult. Suddenly, I feel firmness beneath my feet, making my walking much easier, and I realize the ground is wet. I can feel the sand sticking to my feet and see it covering my toes. Then, a wet coolness washes over my feet as I see waves rolling up to my ankles. Looking up, I see a vast ocean stretching in the bright moonlight. The waves glisten. A bright, white path of reflected moonlight recedes to the horizon. In the black sky is a large, brilliant white moon. I continue to wade into the sea, feeling the water reaching up to my knees. I stop. The ocean spray hits my lips and I taste the salt. The waves rhythmically dash against my knees as I watch them march towards me. I make particular note of their varied sizes and shapes, comparing the amount of white froth that forms on each crest. As the waves hit the shore, they break with a muffled roar. Fascinated, I become lost in feeling the waves wash past my knees and hearing them hit the shore again and again.

In this scene, Bruce starts out *feeling* (his strongest channel) himself in the situation. Then, he bridges from feeling the sand on his feet to seeing it. He does this twice, before bridging from feeling the water at his ankles to seeing the waves. His taste channel is also evoked. The exercise ends with having him bridge to his auditory channel as he listens to the waves break.

By practicing such bridging exercises, Bruce developed the ability to think with all of his channels. He then was able to use a learning trigger to learn and recall material with all three of his main channels, just as Nancy and Max had. His ability to learn company directives and keep up with all the changes at work improved greatly. This made a dramatic improvement in his work performance, earning him the respect of his boss and fellow workers, as well as making his job more fun. He got his raise easily.

HOW TO FIND YOUR DOMINANT CREATIVITY CHANNEL

If you wish to expand your mental power and increase your creativity, first you will need to find out which is your main channel. To do this, simply recall your favorite teacher, your first boss, your colleagues at work, or who served you your most recent meal. If it is easier for you to mentally see someone's face than remember her name or recall the sound of her voice, your main channel is visual. If you first hear her name in your head or imagine her voice, you are auditory. If you first get certain feelings about that person, you are a feeler.

Another way to find your strong channel is to perform the following exercises, which are interesting and fun.

Using only your right hand (left, if you are left-handed), hold your index and second finger together. Then imagine that a strong steel band straps the two together, as a ring that covers both fingers at once. Concentrate only on seeing that steel band as vividly as you can, and as you do that, try to part your fingers. If it is difficult for you to part them until either the image fades away or you remind yourself that it is only an image, you already have good visual powers and are a see-er.

To determine if you are a feeler, instead of visualizing the steel band, imagine the band's cold, hard steel as strongly as you can. As you feel that, try to part your fingers. If this interferes with moving your fingers until you interrupt the imagery with a competing thought (such as dissolving the feeling or reminding yourself that it is not real), you have a good feeling channel.

Finally, to find out if your primary channel is hearing, imagine that a padlock holds the steel band on your fingers. Hear an imaginary click shut and lock your fingers together. If this works to immobilize your fingers until you hear another click release the lock, you are a hearer.

If all of these variations work, you are flexible and skilled in these channels and have no need to do these exercises. If some of them do not work for you, even after you repeat them (being sure to concentrate and dismiss any competing thoughts until you are ready), you need these exercises to expand your thinking abilities. Simply pick a channel that seems to be the strongest for you, and develop further skills by doing these exercises.

HOW TO USE BRIDGING EXERCISES TO STRETCH YOUR IMAGINATION

After deciding which is your main channel, use it as your starting channel in the following exercises. That is, if you are a see-er, start with those exercises that are labeled for those whose main channel is seeing. If you are a hearer, start with those labeled for hearing.

These exercises are designed to create bridges from one of the three main channels to one of the others. With a little practice, this will enable you to think with all of them. The effect is analogous to using physical exercise to strengthen your body. Your improved ability to use a variety of channels will increase your intellectual ability and make your imagination richer. Also, you will find that all of the techniques in this book will work more powerfully for you.

Now select your exercise. Visualizers will start with number I, hearers with II, and feelers with III.

Remember, the key is to imagine with your main channel and, *as you are doing so,* imagine the same thing with a secondary channel. For example, if your main channel is visual, you might imagine the sight of a canary opening his beak. And, using a secondary channel (hearing), you could imagine that you hear him singing.

All that is necessary to do these, or any of the exercises, is concentration and freedom from distraction. Read over the scenes and imagine them from memory, or tape record each one first and play it back while you imagine it as vividly as you can.

Bridging Exercise I: Main Channel Is Seeing

You are in the belfry of an old mission, admiring its rustic architecture and rough-hewn beams. In front of you is an old church bell. It has the character that comes from years of having its shiny brass surface hand-polished. You reach out and place the palm of your hand on this surface, feeling the cool hard metal. You can see the bell's clapper and notice that the bell is about to move. You step back as the bell swings up and strikes against the clapper. As the two metal objects hit each other, you head the loud, resonant peal of the bell. Again the clapper strikes against the rim of the bell, sending out its rich ringing. Although it is loud, you enjoy the interesting reverberations and echoes. Finally it stops, and the world is very still and peaceful.

Bridging Exercise II: Main Channel Is Hearing

You are listening to a live performance of your favorite music and are enjoying this particular arrangement. As you continue to hear the music, look at the instruments and watch them being played, seeing how brightly their colors shine in the spotlight. Now, pick out the sound of one instrument and, as you hear it clearly, watch the musician's fingers work. See the expression and body movement of the player. As you admire his skill, notice the enjoyment inside your body. While you hear the rhythm, feel your foot tap in time with each downbeat, as you continue to enjoy your total immersion in the music.

The next scene can be used in addition to, or instead of, the one that Bruce used, on page 59.

Bridging Exercise III: Main Channel Is Feeling

Feel the hard, tile floor of a shopping center in which you are walking, until you step onto an escalator and sense yourself being carried upward. As you put your hand on the moving banister, see its shiny blackness. Nearing the next level, watch the steps flatten and disappear at the top, just before you step onto the suddenly motionless floor. While you continue to walk among the crowd of shoppers, you can hear the din of their voices. As you pass a couple talking, and watch the woman's lips move, you hear her say, "Then I said to her, 'Mabel.' And then she said . . . " Her voice is shrill. Continue to move among the crowd, hearing snatches of conversations and looking at all the different faces.

After you practice the exercise that starts with your main channel and you become adept at using all three channels, start practicing with the other two exercises that start out in your minor channels. For example, if your main channel is visual and you have practiced with the visual exercise until you are able to easily bridge from visual to auditory and to feeling channels, then practice the exercise that begins with your feeling or hearing channel.

ADVANCED BRIDGING EXERCISES FOR INCREASED CONTROL

The foregoing bridging exercises are the minimum ones needed to expand your mind and personality as described earlier.

Scientific research finds that the ability to control your images is vitally important in creative thinking. Since images are the raw material of imagination and creativity, the more control and skill you have over your images, the more creative you will be. To become even more creative, you should become skillful at multichannel thinking. The following advanced bridging exercises are designed to help you do this.

The next set of exercises teach you to exclude various channels. When you exclude mental channels, the remaining ones become more vivid and powerful. For instance, speed readers do not use their verbal channel to sound out the words in their head as they read. They take in the written information visually. This system is much faster.

Many creative activities, at certain times in the process of creation, need to have only one channel highlighted. When a composer is creating music, for instance, she needs her auditory channel in action. Then her feeling channel needs to be used to include the right emotional tone in the music, and then her verbal channel is needed to write the music on paper. During the heat of creation, a composer will switch back and forth among these channels from moment to moment as needed. She does this unconsciously. And so will you be able to use your channels without having to think about them. When you develop your mental channels adequately, they will be at your disposal spontaneously.

To increase you control over the images, practice the following exercises. Again, read these over just before you began the exercise or make a tape recording of each one to play back.

Exercise Excluding Your Visual Channel

Imagine that it is pitch dark and you are lying in bed in a strange house. Feel the texture of the sheets, the firmness of the mattress, the softness of the pillow. The smell of spring flowers is strong in the room. The night is cool and you enjoy the comforting warmth of your blanket. As you move your body, you can hear the rustle of the sheets. There is a ticking sound that continues rhythmically. It is joined by a steady droning noise from outside that lulls you into a sense of profound peace as you lie in utter blackness.

Exercise Excluding Your Feeling Channel

You are in a large barn enjoying a glass of cold, zesty apple cider. As you look up into the high ceiling, the smell of fresh-mown hay fills your nostrils. Suddenly a load of hay in the middle of the aisle bursts into flame, blocking your exit. The smell of smoke is strong. As you watch the flames dance and the sparks fly, and hear the burning wood crackle and spit, you realize you do not feel any heat. You step closer but still feel nothing. Fascinated, you stretch out your hand and place it at the edge of the flame. There is still no heat, nor is your hand or sleeve burned. You keep on approaching and feel nothing; You walk right through the flames in total comfort and safety. Once outside, you watch the entire barn burn to cinders. By then it is night, and you lose yourself while gazing into the red embers.

Many of my clients report an enjoyable sense of power and invulnerability after exercising this particular scene.

Finally, in the next exercise, we will exclude your hearing channel.

Exercise Excluding Your Hearing Channel

Imagine yourself watching an old, silent movie. You are alone in the theater and it is very quiet. You do not hear anything. Watch the movie in detail. It is exciting. You can feel your heart beating, and you become aware of the rising and falling of your chest as you breathe. You have some hot buttered popcorn and its smell starts your saliva flowing. As you start eating, you can feel its texture. It tastes delicious and you feel the pleasure in your mouth and stomach. Finally, the movie ends, you leave your seat, and start walking up the aisle toward the exit. Two men approach you, and you can see them talking together with much animation. As they pass by, you realize you cannot hear them. They are like actors in a silent movie. When you come to the lobby doors of heavy glass, it is daylight and you can look out into the busy street, with people and cars hurrying by. You open the door and step out. Everything is still—completely silent. It is cold and windy. To protect yourself, you draw up your coat and lean into the wind to keep your balance. You walk through a silent city, enjoying the sights, which uncluttered by sound, are sharp and clear.

Practice these exercises until you can evoke each channel clearly in your mind. If for some reason the content of these scenes are uncomfortable for you, you can design your own, using the principle of bridging. For instance, if you do not like escalators or shopping centers, substitute something you enjoy. Instead of an escalator, imagine the feeling of standing in a refreshing mountain stream as you watch the water flow by your feet. And as you watch the water, you hear it splash.

When you use enjoyable subjects in this way, these exercises are very pleasant and provide a side benefit of relaxing you mentally and physically. As you know, stress reduction promotes good health. Also, after finishing a session, you will be refreshed and have new energy.

BRIDGING EXERCISES TO PROVIDE A WELLSPRING OF CREATIVE POWERS THAT YOU CAN DRAW FROM INSTANTLY

The most creative thinking arrives at solutions never thought of before. Dr. Flemming, the discoverer of penicillin, could see things in new ways. He was not the first scientist to observe the green mold. Others saw it as a nuisance that ruined their germ cultures. Flemming saw it as a cure for human infection.

The ability to think with abstract images is especially effective for providing novel ideas and approaches. You will not be situation bound and you will be able to think of things in new ways.

To help you gain this creative ability, I've included a special set of bridging exercises that do not use scenes, but use abstract objects instead.

These exercises should be practiced as the preceding ones. Begin with your main channel.

Visual Abstract Exercise

Picture a sphere in front of you. You can make it any size you wish. Then imagine what color it is. As it becomes bright and clear, imagine what kind of sound it might make, and as you continue to watch, listen to it making that sound. Then have it pass through your body, perhaps from the top of your head and out through your left foot. As you watch this happening, feel the sensations it makes. Imagine what the object smells and tastes like.

Next, imagine another geometric figure. See its shape and give it a color, as you feel it pass it through another part of your body. Smell and taste it.

Keep choosing different shapes, colors, and sounds, and pass these through your body, having them enter and leave your body from different directions. Smell and taste them.

Do this for fifteen to twenty minutes at a session, until you can do it easily and well.

Now you are ready for the next exercise variation. This starts with sound, bridges to vision, then to feelings, and ends with taste and smell.

Imagine a beautiful sound and the color you want it to be. Then give it whatever shape seems right to you. When you hear and see this clearly in front of you, pass it through your body and feel its journey. Lastly, smell and taste this object.

Continue doing this with various sounds, as you did with various shapes in the previous exercise. When you have mastered this variation, you are ready to go on to the next.

The final variation starts with your feeling channel, bridges to your visual channel and then goes on to your auditory one.

Focus your attention on feelings of peace and serenity as you relax. Imagine what color goes with such feelings. Then imagine what form it would take, and what sounds would come from it. Pass this out in front of you and look at it, studying and meditating on your creation. Give it a smell and then a taste.

Continue with this variation. Become aware of some sensation in your body (such as the weight of your hand on your lap). Then, as you did above, imagine what color that sensation would be, what shape, what sounds fit it. Move this out of your body and place it in front of you, and watch and listen to it, noticing all its nuances of color, shape and sound. Lastly smell and taste it.

Practice this process (of starting with a feeling and bridging to the other channels) until you can do it well.

After you are able to do all these exercises well, you will find yourself able to use your mind more powerfully. The special strengths of each channel will be available for you and creative ideas will occur more readily.

FOUR STEPS TO GREATER CREATIVITY

After you able to do all these exercises well, you will find yourself able to use your mind more powerfully. The special strengths of each channel will be available for you and ideas will occur more readily when doing creative activities.

Researchers have found that there are four stages you go through when being creative. First, you *prepare* by gathering information and images. This is a conscious process. You focus on your goal: the problem to be solved or the outcome you want. Then you collect all the relevant data you can.

After strengthening your channels with the exercises I have been describing, your mind will be much more versatile and effective because you will be gathering and storing information in all your channels.

The second stage is *incubation*. Release conscious hold of the problem. Allow the answer simply to happen. Don't judge the process and free yourself from habitual thoughts and ideas. Daydreams, night dreams, relaxation, self-hypnosis, and the bridging exercises are conducive to your unconscious mind working out a solution.

Have faith that the answer will come. Your increased ability to bridge between channels will dramatically increase the chances that you will make novel connections between the words, sounds, pictures, feelings, and even smells and tastes that you have been collecting.

The third stage is *illumination.* Suddenly, seemingly from nowhere, a solution presents itself. With all five channels now strengthened their contributions will be greater. Accept whatever idea comes, including concrete symbols and abstract ideas. Great moments in creativity are associated with images occurring spontaneously in one or two channels. Your other channels will have made their input on an unconscious level. For instance, you may consciously see a solution that has been worked out with the help of your feeling channel working outside your awareness to find what fits and feels right.

The final stage is *verification.* In your imagination, test out whether the solution works and take out any kinks needed to make the idea workable. Again, with five strong channels, the kinks will be more obvious and ways to take them out more readily forthcoming. This stage, like the first, is conscious, while the middle stages are both unconscious.

Besides helping you be much more creative when using the general techniques just cited, developing powerful channels will help you be more effective with all imagery methods, including the techniques that are given throughout this book.

5

Mental Blueprints: How To Use Triggers To Improve Your Performance and Master New Skills

Mendel grew some peas. Freud talked to some unhappy women. Darwin watched some birds. Each of these seemingly mundane activities were the basis for far-reaching discoveries about nature and mankind. Now, certain athletes get a glazed look in their eyes and do a little daydreaming at particular times during their sport. Certain patients, with serious physical diseases, also get the same glazed look and have their own daydreams. Will equally important discoveries come from this? Evidence is mounting that they will.

HOW "IMAGINATION POWER" HAS BEEN PROVEN TO STIMULATE PEAK PERFORMANCES

Some researchers took three groups of basketball players to test out if practicing a skill in your imagination—mental rehearsal— could improve your ability to do that skill in real life. Most scientists doubted imaginary practice would make any difference, but others thought it might help a little. They were astounded with the results of the experiment.

Each group was scored on the percent of baskets they could shoot. Then, over the next twenty days, one group did nothing, another group practiced shooting real baskets for twenty minutes each day, and the last group practiced shooting baskets only in their *imagination* for the same time periods as the second group. When all the groups were reassembled in the gym at the end of the twenty days, they were tested to see if they could improve on their original scores. Those who did nothing did not improve. As expected, those who actually practiced improved. However, those who only practiced in their imagination improved too. Not only that, their rate of improvement was as good as those who practiced in real life. Imagination practice proved to be equally as effective, at a statistically significant level, as real practice.

Think of it. Mentally rehearsing or practicing in your easy chair can be as helpful as practicing in real life, such as on the basketball court.

Professional and serious amateur athletes all over the world are taking advantage of mental rehearsal. Many athletes in the Olympic games use imagery techniques to improve their game. Steffi Martin, Bettina Schmidt, and Ute Weiss are East German women athletes who dominated the 1984 luge competition (racing against the clock on a single-person sled down an icy corkscrew chute at speeds well over sixty miles per hour). In the luge race, the turns have to be made perfectly—not only to avoid a disastrous spill, but to hit each curve at the exact angle to maintain maximum speed.

The announcer of the television broadcast of this event explained that each woman mentally rehearsed the demanding course just before they started. If you watched their faces on that broadcast, you could see each one of them doing this. When sitting on her sled before the start, Steffi Martin's eyes glazed over for about a minute during her mental rehearsal. Then with breathless speed and agility, she guided her sled to victory. You could watch both Schmidt and Weiss mentally rehearse the same way.

These three women made a clean sweep—winning the gold, silver, and bronze medals.

Similarly, U.S.A.'s William Carow used imagery techniques. He talked about these techniques on television at the site of these games in Sarajevo, Yugoslavia.

Carow's sport was the Biathlon, a grueling contest that demanded speed, endurance, and fine muscle control. He skied cross country over six miles at top speed. At specified intervals along the course, he was required to stop, take his rifle off his back, and shoot at five targets before continuing on. For every miss, he would be penalized. Imagine, after skiing for miles, your body all keyed up and breathing heavily from your exertions, being required to settle down quickly and steel your nerves to squeeze off five accurate shots. Carow was able to use his imagery training to slow immediately his breathing and heart rate to steady his body. He hit every target.

These demonstrations of imagination power have mind-boggling ramifications, especially when you also take into account the work being done in some hospitals to have patients use their imagination to help heal themselves. Significant recoveries have been achieved using these mental healing techniques. (Exactly how you can use your imagination to help heal yourself is explained in Chapter 6.)

The evidence adds up to one unavoidable conclusion: Your mind and body respond in extremely important ways to your imagination.

Exactly how this happens is unclear. We don't know, of course, just how our thoughts move our body—how does the decision to raise an arm actually cross the ephemeral realm of ideas and activate the concrete realm of the physical? How do we raise our arm? How do our thoughts about ourselves affect our actual physical being and behavior?

The cerebral cortex is believed to be the seat of consciousness. Consciousness implies voluntary behavior. So when we think, the voluntary thoughts we form in this higher brain center are accompanied by electrochemical activity which filters down to the midbrain (the cerebrum) and the lower brain (the brain stem). These parts of the brain control our physical functioning, including movement, muscle coordination, and homeostasis—the housekeeping functions of the body such as temperature control, waste elimination, hormone levels, and healing.

A negative thought sends a noxious electrochemical stimulation, and the lower brain reacts to these by giving negative commands to our body. But if we think a positive thought, it produces a positive stimulation which makes the lower brain centers react by giving positive commands to our body. It is as if our thoughts send down a blueprint to be followed.

This presents us with many exciting possibilities. Just by imagining the right things—providing the proper blueprint—you can induce profound changes in yourself.

Although sports enthusiasts might disagree strongly, using imagery techniques just to improve your game is of minor importance when compared to applying these principles to improve your total well being and achieve your life's goals. However, imagery techniques in sports are worth exploring because sports readily lend themselves to scientific investigation.

Racers can be clocked to thousands of a second, bowling and golf scores have uniform units of measurement for scoring, diving and figure skating have a systematic way of observing and measuring performance.

MULTICHANNEL IMAGERY IS MUCH MORE POWERFUL THAN VISUALIZATION

Early researchers had their subjects only visualize when doing their mental rehearsal. They got some good results and "visualization" became a catchword. Unfortunately, this led many people to neglect the power of other channels.

Now, from our newer research with sports, we have learned that there is more to imagery techniques than visualizing. The way you imagine makes a big difference. Sometimes mentally hearing or feeling is more effective than visualizing in improving your skills through mental rehearsal.

Also, combining several channels when mentally rehearsing is always more powerful than using only one channel. Multichannel imagery, sometimes called total imagery, provides even better results than visualizing.

For example, concentrating on your weaker channel improves performance. Athletes who are see-ers did better by paying more attention to their feeling channel. Bowlers, who thought mostly with their visual channel, could let this channel work automatically and concentrate on feeling how their bodies worked as they played. They paid attention to such things as their rhythm as they approached the alley, how far back they swung the ball, and the feeling of throwing the ball and following through. Conversely, those bowlers whose main channel was feeling paid visual attention to their angle of approach to the alley and to aiming the ball.

In addition to using several channels, there are other factors that increase the effectiveness of mental practice.

At Cornell University, psychologists Ulric Neisser and Georgia Nigro have demonstrated that different results occur depending on the vantage point from which you imagine yourself playing. If you watch yourself from the sidelines, you get a different result than if you imagine yourself right in the game. Watching yourself improves form—the way you look when playing, which would be important to a figure skater. Imagining yourself right in the game improves performance. You hit more bull's eyes.

Another imagery technique is *modeling:* copying someone who already has the skills you want to acquire. This can be someone you know and have a chance to observe or it can be someone on television.

This gives us four powerful principles to consider when doing mental practice: model your target behavior after someone, use multichannel imagery, imagine yourself performing from the right vantage point, and concentrate on your weaker channel.

HOW JIM DRAMATICALLY IMPROVED HIS GOLF WITH THE MENTAL BLUEPRINT TECHNIQUE

Jim, a client of mine, improved his golf game ten strokes by using a technique based on the foregoing principles, called the Mental Blueprint. He watched his favorite pro golfer on television and then practiced hitting the ball entirely in his imagination while sitting in his favorite easy chair at home.

Jim used the Mental Blueprint technique in this way. First, he imagined seeing himself, as if he was watching a movie of himself, swing just like the pro. When he could do this, he then stepped into the picture and, from this new viewpoint, imagined it again. He not only saw what it looked like from this perspective, but also felt what a good swing was like. He also imagined the sound of his club whistling through the air and the satisfying smack of the club head solidly meeting the ball. This engaged three of his channels. To engage a fourth channel, he even added the smell of the lush grass at the course where he golfed. Each imagery session lasted about one half hour and he practiced this two or three times a week. (He only needed to refresh his image of the pro's swing by watching him about once a month, however.)

When he was playing on the golf course, Jim used the other important refinement for playing better—concentrating on your weak channel. Jim's weakest channel was feeling, so he concentrated on being aware of how his swing felt. (His strong channel, sight, automatically worked without his attention.) He was delighted with the improvement in his game.

Here is an outline of the Mental Blueprint for improving your game by installing new skills in yourself or keeping your present skills sharp.

If you are not sports-minded, use a little physical game, like pitching pennies, to test this technique.

The Mental Blueprint: Nine Steps for Improving Physical Skills

1. Decide what skill you want to practice. Then, use three channels in your imagination.
2. Study your models.
3. From a distance, see and hear yourself performing the desired sport.
4. Step into the picture and repeat the scene.
5. If it doesn't feel right, step outside the scene and adjust your actions.
6. Go into the picture again and repeat it.
7. If it feels right, then create a trigger. Discard those behaviors that you cannot make feel right.
8. Imagine yourself in future scenes, firing your trigger and engaging in your new skills.
9. When really playing, concentrate on using your weaker channel.

Step 8 intends for you to imagine yourself as if you are in the game. However, if you engage in a sport like diving or figure skating, where you want to look good to an outside observer, such as a judge or audience, it is equally important to also imagine viewing yourself, as in step 3.

With this method, you can improve your golf, bowling, tennis, or whatever it is you like to play, right in the comfort of your home. Simply use the Mental Blueprint technique for whatever activity you wish to improve. Make a trigger so you can recreate the attitude and feeling you had during the programming session. Use whomever you can as a model: the best player on your team, someone on television —or recall the times you played exceptionally well and be your own model. Any skill requires practice, but, with this method, you can do much of your practice in your mind and still reap the benefits of improved performance. This can be especially useful when you need to save time or your equipment is inaccessible.

HOW YOU CAN USE GOLD MEDAL WINNING TECHNIQUES TO IMPROVE YOUR LIFE

You can also use these techniques to improve your life. My experience with clients shows these techniques to be equally powerful when used to master other skills.

A young man learned the latest dances using the Mental Blueprint technique. He watched the best dancers and then mentally rehearsed, using the nine-step system. He was able to rapidly become adept at each new dance by practicing in his imagination. When he stepped on the dance floor with a partner, he was already proficient. He became a much sought-after dance partner, and this helped him to achieve a full social life.

An ambitious actor used these techniques to master a wide range of roles. Although he could rehearse out loud, he found the Mental Blueprint invaluable because he could use mental rehearsal when traditional rehearsal was impractical. He would mentally rehearse while waiting at airports, the doctor's office, and at other times when his time would have been otherwise wasted. This efficient use of his time gave him an edge in the highly competitive acting field. He could have his role highly polished by the time auditions were held.

In addition, step 3 was especially helpful to him. He used it to create a powerful performance. From the viewpoint of the audience, he would imagine himself play his role. Then he would adjust this image until it had just the right emotional impact.

He personally credits these techniques with helping him win a prestigious acting award and enjoying a highly successful career.

An automotive engineer, who had come up the hard way, used

the Mental Blueprint to overcome blocks to his career. He was a brilliant engineer, but his career was being frustrated. He wanted to rise in the executive ranks, but doors were closed to him because his manner and speech were coarse. Unfortunately, at the higher corporate levels, fitting in socially with the other executives plays an important role in getting promoted.

Our coarse-mannered engineer used the Mental Blueprint technique to change his social behavior — his manners, the vocabulary he used, the way he dressed, and his diction — so he would look and sound like his colleagues. In a remarkably short time, he smoothed the rough edges of his social personality. It wasn't long before he won a key promotion, assuring a successful career based on his engineering and managerial abilities.

Another benefit he enjoyed was being included socially with the men he worked with. After his change, they no longer avoided him. They chatted with him informally and ate lunch together. He and his family were invited to dinners and outings. Up until then, it had been lonely for him and he had coped with the social isolation by claiming that it didn't bother him. However, he had to admit that his new acceptance by his fellow workers made his job even more satisfying.

HOW MARCIA USED THE MENTAL BLUEPRINT TO REV UP HER SOCIAL LIFE

The achievement of social skills is one of the more significant uses for the Mental Blueprint.

Marcia was a lonely single woman who rarely dated. Her social life was barren. After using the Mental Blueprint, she became a much sought-after partner and her life became filled with fun and excitement. She eventually chose one of her many admirers and married.

However, when she first came to see me, she was very lonely. Panic was setting in because she was fast approaching her fortieth birthday and she feared life was going to pass her by. She was depressed and spoke through clenched teeth to keep from crying.

Although basically a good-looking woman, her clothes and hair were both severely styled, and her cosmetics were underdone. You had to look closely to appreciate her good looks. Her character was sterling—honest and reliable. She had a good job as an assistant manager of a department store, and her boss valued her work highly. She was a good tennis and bridge player, and a good conversationalist.

Step 1. Decide What New Behavior You Want to Learn

Marcia didn't know how to attract men. Somehow she turned them off. Rather than going through the tedious job of finding out how she did this, we decided she should learn the necessary social skills for appropriately attracting them.

To learn these new skills, we developed a Mental Blueprint technique that omitted step nine of the sports version.

This technique uses two modes: visually imaging yourself from outside and inside the mental picture. The first mode provides *detachment*, a calm, contemplative attitude that helps you learn because you are detached from emotions that may cloud your thinking. Detachment is accomplished by imagining seeing yourself from a distance. You can see your own face just as if you were watching a movie of yourself.

The second mode is emotional involvement. This checks out whether your behavior is essentially in accord with all parts of your personality. This is accomplished by stepping into the picture and imagining it from that perspective. When you step into the picture this way, you can feel whether the behavior you imagine is comfortable. Since the integrity of your personality is important—you should feel proud of what you do—if the new behavior does not feel right, you will need to try other behaviors. Also, to be effective, your imaginary new behavior has to be believable to you.

How these two modes work will become clearer as I describe how Marcia used them.

Step 2. Study Your Models

I began teaching her the Mental Blueprint technique by asking her a question: "Who are some women you admire for the way they relate to men—women you think you could learn from and could adapt some of their behaviors into your own personality? It can be women you know personally, as well as celebrities. These are your models."

She told me of three who fit that description. She decided personal friends or acquaintances were better because she could observe them more intimately in surroundings that were natural to her. Many of the Hollywood scenarios—such as a millionairess attracting a private eye—weren't very useful to Marcia.

"Concentrate," I continued, "and see and hear these women relating to men in your imagination. Also imagine what they are feeling as they do this. Notice the way they dress, use cosmetics, style their hair, how they act around men, how they handle their bodies, the expression on their faces, what they say, their tone of voice, the way they smell, and anything else that seems relevant to you. Give yourself all the time you need to study them."

She closed her eyes to concentrate better and after several minutes opened them to report, "I see a lot of things they do that I don't do. I'm not sure I can do those things."

Step 3. From a Distance, See and Hear Yourself Performing the Desired Behavior

"Trust yourself. You will be able to do most of them. We will sort out which ones you can do.

"Now," I continued, "imagine watching yourself doing the same things those women do to attract men. This is the first mode: detachment," I went on. "It is as if you are the director of a movie in which you are the star. Rehearse all the different approaches these women use. When you look and sound good to yourself, let me know."

She closed her eyes again, but for a little longer this time. When she opened them, she described how she saw herself dressing and acting more like these women.

"I just realized something," she said. "When I imagine myself acting like these successful women, I'm not trying to show men how smart or competent I am. Normally, I'm concerned that they will think I'm dumb and I try to impress them and start competing with them."

"That sounds like you learned something," I answered.

Step 4. Step into the Picture and Repeat the Scene

"Now use the second mode," I continued, "and step into the

picture. Repeat the behavior from this new perspective. Not only see and hear the experience, but notice how it feels to you."

After doing this, she reported, "It doesn't feel right at all to be loud and talkative like Harriet. But I like the way she dresses best of any of them."

"If being loud does not feel good to you, either modify it or forget it. Keep only those behaviors that feel right to you."

"Okay," Marcia said. "I'll dress like Harriet. But I notice quiet little Mary gets all the men she wants. Actually, she has complained to me she has trouble getting rid of boyfriends. I'll mentally rehearse being like her."

After rehearsing in her imagination for a while, Marcia said, "It doesn't feel right being as self-effacing as she is. But I sure like her sweetness, caring heart, and sensitivity to others' feelings."

Step 5. If It Doesn't Feel Right, Step Outside the Scene and Adjust Your Actions

"Keep what you like. You can modify the behavior until it feels right."

"What do you mean when you say, 'It should feel right'?" asked Marcia.

"I mean, when you imagine yourself acting in the new ways, it should feel reasonably comfortable and believable to you. It's important that you can believe it's possible for you to act in the new ways.

"To change your behavior until it feels right, first step out of the picture and become the director again. Change your behavior until it looks like what you want."

Step 6. Go into the Picture Again and Repeat It

"When these adjusted behaviors look right," I continued, "try out how they feel by again stepping back into the picture. Discard those behaviors that you cannot make feel believable. Keep the rest."

She did so and told me she made herself less self-effacing but not competitive like she used to be. She saw herself relating on an "I'm-OK, you're-OK," basis. This felt acceptable to her.

Step 7. When It Feels Right, Create a Trigger

"Now that you have imagined a satisfactory new behavior," I

told her, "create a trigger for it that you can fire whenever you want to use your new behavior in a real social situation."

Step 8. Imagine Yourself in Future Scenes, Firing Your Trigger and Engaging in Your New Responses

After she made her trigger, I had her mentally rehearse her target: acting in her new ways and enjoying herself as she successfully attracted men friends. She reported that this scene felt believable to her.

"Rehearse this often and put them into real-life practice at the first opportunity," I told her.

Sometime later, when I last saw Marcia, she was radiant. She was attractively groomed, and I was impressed by how attractive she had made herself appear.

I was even more impressed by her confident, easily smiling manner and what she told me about her new life. She started getting dates and then began to have problems similar to Mary, one of the women she had modeled after. Marcia had to decide which boy-friends to choose — there were too many to go out with all of them. At last, she did choose. She showed me her engagement ring — a beautiful large solitaire.

In contrast to Marcia's old-fashioned approach to man-woman relationships, a woman in her early thirties used this trigger technique to ask men out on dates. She had had a small town, traditional upbringing that stressed a passive role for women. Now she wanted to change her responses and deal with men on an equal footing. The Mental Blueprint technique enabled her to do this easily and graciously, avoiding much of the awkward situations that can arise when trying out something new without practicing first.

She was delighted with her new abilities. Her self-respect and sense of control over her life increased enormously. Life took on a new dimension and became more satisfying.

Here is an outline of the version of the Mental Blueprint that is modified for installing social skills in yourself. Using another person to model your behavior after is optional. You might have a sufficiently clear idea of how you want to act so you will not need one.

The Mental Blueprint: Eight Steps for Mastering Social Skills

1. Decide what new behavior you want to learn. Then, using three channels in your imagination:
2. Study your models.
3. From a distance, see and hear yourself performing the desired behavior.
4. Step into the picture and repeat the scene.
5. If it doesn't feel right, step outside the scene and adjust your actions.
6. Go into the picture again and repeat it.
7. When it feels right, create a trigger.
8. Imagine yourself in future scenes, firing your trigger and engaging in your new responses.

As you can see, you can think of making mental blueprints as directing a movie in which you are at first the director, directing yourself as the principle actor. Then when you think you have it right, you become the actor, seeing the scene through the actor's eyes and getting a feeling for the situation you are now in.

You can use this system for any new behavior you want to add to your repertoire. As we saw, an actor improved his performance, an engineer polished his social skills and ended the prejudices that were blocking his promotions, Marcia changed her whole life from dullness to excitement by using it to reprogram herself to act in ways that men find attractive, while a young woman changed her dating style to a more active one and found the kind of gratifications she valued.

6

How To Trigger Your Mental Pentagon To Help Heal Illness and Maintain Vigorous Health

Psychology has always been an important part of the healing arts. In his writings, ancient Greek physician Hippocrates recognized that the attitude of a patient influences the outcome of his or her treatment. If the patient should become discouraged and "give up," he or she will generally do poorly, or may even die. Feelings of helplessness and futility are especially devastating — but not only for those who are already ill; negative thoughts invite illness in the healthy.

As mentioned in Chapter 5, some hospitals, in addition to regular medical treatment, are directing patients to imagine their bodies healing.

THE BRAIN AS HEALER

Researchers at the National Institutes of Health have laboratory evidence of the mind's power to heal your body. They discovered that certain brain chemicals are present when subjects are in a positive mood. These chemicals attract macrophages — your body's disease-fighting cells—to injured tissue. The macrophages attack and destroy disease causing germs and other agents.

Since your moods are largely controlled by what you think, scientists believe such findings indicate that your disease-fighting immune system can be consciously controlled. Since images are the language of the brain, imaging is a powerful way to enlist the aid of your immune system.

It goes deeper than being in a good mood, as important as that is. Modern science is discovering specifically how a patient's thinking can profoundly influence his recovery.

Carl and Stephanie Simonton, of the Cancer Counseling Research Center in Fort Worth, have done outstanding research in this area. This husband-and-wife team have demonstrated that patients who imagined their body ridding itself of cancer (while also undergoing conventional medical treatment) did significantly better than those who did not. The imaginers suffered less, responded better to treatment, their hospital stays were shorter, and a greater number of them recovered.

The Simontons' studies demonstrate that your thoughts are a significant force in helping you to get better faster, more completely, and more often. Also, spontaneous remissions (those most welcome but mysterious disappearances of deadly disease) are more frequent.

We have long been intrigued by spontaneous remissions. They occur without warning or hint of how or why they happen. I remember, as a young man, attending the retirement party of a colleague. He was a slender 65-year-old man with white, wavy hair who carried himself with the air of "elder statesman." At the gathering, Ralph gave us a little farewell talk. I was surprised when he told us he had had cancer some fifteen years earlier. The surgeons had opened him up for exploratory surgery, taken one look at the massive spread of the disease, sewed him up, and sent him home to die. His case seemed so hopeless, the only treatment they offered him were narcotics to ease the pain. Yet he amazed everyone by recovering completely. Ralph offered us no explanation. He said he had none. "It just went away."

Then—as if it were of no consequence—he added a most interesting afterthought, "It was a dream come true."

It's as if there is a positive force deep inside us that is simply waiting for direction, like a general in the master command post waiting for orders. We need to communicate with that "general." In Ralph's dreams of getting well, he had unconsciously communicated with that mysterious inner force.

The mental blueprints described in the previous chapter are not only able to guide our voluntary behavior system; they also profoundly influence our involuntary bodily processes that control vital functioning, such as physical growth, energy, and health. Imagery is a powerful way of communicating with this positive force.

It could well be that the key to the mystery of spontaneous remission lies in such communication. So far, the two known methods of influencing spontaneous remissions are imagery (with or without hypnosis) and faith healing. Someday, as our techniques become even more refined, we may be able to influence remissions to occur more frequently.

There is a large body of evidence that suggests that merely taking time out to think of essentially neutral things benefits your body. For example, many meditative techniques simply have you concentrate on your breathing, a nonsense word, or counting backwards. In themselves, these thoughts do not directly imply any particular outcome (such as healing or growing calmer). But a positive outcome is implied in their use. Lectures often given before learning a meditation method tell of the rewards to be expected from following the regime. So meditation is not completely neutral because these preliminary comments act as suggestions.

HOW POSITIVE THOUGHTS HELP HEAL YOUR BODY

Although using a neutral idea (such as repeatedly thinking a nonsense word) has demonstrable healing effects, using specific, clearly positive thoughts has more powerful healing effects. For example, instead of imagining the word *one* repeatedly, you can visualize parts of your body healing. Studies have shown that this method results in a higher percentage of recoveries from illness. Even more powerful results are achieved by using imagery with multiple channels, such as seeing, hearing and feeling your body heal itself.

Although, in Chapter 5, I spoke of our thoughts as a blueprint for our bodies to follow, we should realize that, since a blueprint essentially provides visual information, the term *blueprint* connotes only the visual aspect of imagination. The blueprint metaphor does not take into account the importance of imagining with all five channels. To convey the contribution of all our channels, instead of a blueprint, we can think of our model of mental healing more accurately as a five-point star—a guiding star.

CHANNELS

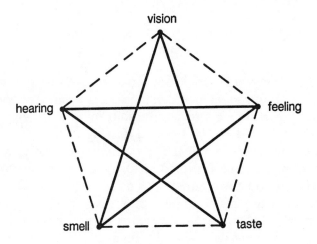

Each of its points represents a channel. Connecting all of the points of the star forms a pentagon, a symbol that man has pondered upon since antiquity. Our collective unconscious has sensed the power of our channels all along, influencing the ancients to attribute mystical power to the five-point star, as well as to the pentagon.

It is only now that modern science is removing the mystery and uncovering the tremendous influence our five channels have on us. As explained in earlier chapters, researchers are finding that multichannel imagining turns your mind into a virtual learning machine, profoundly expands your creativity, and makes mental practice an amazingly effective way to gain new skills and abilities. Clearly, multichannel imagining makes imagery methods more powerful.

It comes as no surprise then, that using your mind to heal your body also is greatly enhanced with multichannel thinking. The mind is a wonderful healing mechanism when used properly.

William D. Fezler, associate director of the Institute for Comprehensive Medicine in Beverly Hills, California, has written about the potent effects of imagining in all five senses. He finds that all healing is greatly enhanced this way.

Prominent researcher J. R. Cautela has also investigated the power of multichannel thinking. In *The Power of Human Imagination*, he uses the term *sense modalities* in place of "mental channels." He writes, "The greatest effectiveness (is) when a client reports vividness in *all sense modalities* (italics mine)."

HOW TO USE YOUR MENTAL PENTAGON TO DIRECT YOUR PERSONAL WAR AGAINST DISEASE

You can direct your own personal war against diseases invading your body. With our greater understanding of channel power, you can design powerful weapons within your mind and help yourself get well. This is called *Mental Imagery Healing*.

During their early work, the Simontons used only the visual channel and instructed patients to picture their cancer being cured. They could do this in any manner that suited their fancy. One patient would imagine seeing his cancer as dragons being hacked to death by an armored knight. Another would picture his illness more literally as malformed cells being weakened by medicines and then eaten by white blood cells. The patients would practice their imagery throughout the day.

Regardless of what the content of their imagery was, as long as the symbol representing cancer was defeated, the Simontons got impressive results with these patients. More of the patients who used it got well—even some who were medically deemed to be hopeless —compared to patients who did not use mental healing. (This may sound unbelievable, but Pasteur's discovery that many diseases are caused by our bodies being invaded by tiny animals too small to be seen by the unaided eye must have seemed unbelievable too.)

However, some patients just couldn't use their visual channel. They did not know how. This left these patients out of the program.

We now have two solutions for patients who do not visualize well: They can use the bridging exercises in Chapter 4 to expand their minds so they can visualize, or they can imagine in other channels. This refinement allows many more patients to use the amazing healing powers of their mind.

For example, a patient who cannot make mental pictures could use his hearing channel to imagine the sound of his cancer being chopped to pieces, ground up, or exploded.

A variant of the sound channel is to form words in your mind, such as "my body is healing." Such self-talk is effective. You may recognize that giving yourself such verbal suggestions is similar to the famous phrase of the nineteenth-century hypnotist, Coé: "Everyday, in every way, I am getting better and better."

Instead of, or in addition to, your visual or sound channel, you can use your feeling channel. For example, you could imagine feeling the cancer draining out of your body, or feel it shrinking to nothing.

Of course, we now understand that using additional channels makes Mental Imagery Healing more effective. So use as many channels as you can and develop the ability to use them all. Practice the bridging exercises, if necessary, so you can see, hear, and feel your illness being defeated.

Besides being effective in helping to cure cancer, these same Mental Healing methods work on other illnesses. In California, Errol R. Korn, M.D., uses the same principles to hasten his patients' recovery from such severe neurologic injuries as stroke or spinal cord damage.

He combines mental practice with standard rehabilitation therapy and has evidence that this not only reduces recovery time by half, but probably produces better results. Patients on his program seem to recover more completely. They have greater mobility and strength in their once-paralyzed limbs.

Dr. Korn uses hypnosis to help his patients achieve a state of relaxed concentration. Working with one patient whose nervous system injury caused her to lose the ability to swallow, he directed her to imagine swallowing her favorite malts and hamburgers. As a result, she learned how to swallow in just two days. With only traditional treatment, his records indicate that most patients with similar conditions take over fourteen days to learn this.

Dr. Korn has brought about significant improvements in about three quarters of the patients he's treated with imagery techniques.

Using hypnosis with the imagery techniques is optional. The combination helps some patients recover faster and more fully than simply using imagery alone. Although Korn uses hypnosis, the Simontons do not. Also, the Simontons teach their patients to guide their own images so they can practice on their own.

In addition to guided imagery helping patients heal themselves of cancer and neurological illness, guided imagery also helps victims of other diseases. Impressive results have been reported by patients directing their own images.

HOW JANICE USED HER MENTAL PENTAGON TO COMBAT A RAGING INFECTION

Janice had an inner ear infection that was responding too slowly to antibiotics. Before she started her health images, she had already gone through twice the amount of medicine that normally cures this problem. But her ear was still aching. She was getting worried, afraid she might develop a strain of germs that was impervious to antibiotics. An infection raging out of control would be serious, especially because the site of the infection was near her brain.

She started a third source of antibiotics. If this did not work . . . well, she didn't want to think about that. At this point, she began using multiple-channel imagery, imagining that her inner ear was red with inflammation and being painted with white paint. The paint felt cool and soothing as it was "applied." Since she always associated the smell of iodine with strong healing power, she imagined the paint smelling like iodine, "very mediciney." She practiced imagining this twice a day for twenty minutes. Her earache almost disappeared the first session. In three days, she was symptom-free. After her doctor took her off antibiotics this time, she had no relapses.

You will notice that Janice used her visual channel and then bridged to feeling and smelling. On the other hand, Sam was a patient who used his feeling channel by imagining his aching arthritic joints being bathed in a warm and slippery fluid. He also imagined them becoming smooth. This gave him considerable relief. Another arthritic patient, Julie, got similar results imagining coolness instead of heat, because, for her, coolness always made her joints feel better.

HOW JOHN CONTROLLED HIS IRRITABLE COLON THROUGH MENTAL HEALING AND BECAME AN ACTIVE MAN AGAIN

Whenever John felt stressed, such as when he was working hard, his colon would act up and he would be miserable. He was getting depressed. "I'm tired of pampering myself," he confided in me, "but this problem just keeps nagging at me until I quit and take it easy. I'm never going to get ahead in my business."

When John met me, he was skeptical of mental healing. Earlier, he had gone to a respected therapist for help with his irritable colon. But the therapist had tried to get John to use visual images. Unfortunately, John's visual channel was weak and he couldn't picture things in his mind, so he didn't benefit from trying such guided imagery.

However, when I told him about multichannel thinking, he discovered his auditory verbal channel was his strong one. He learned to calm himself by relaxing and repeating the word *calm* and telling himself his colon was healing. Much like the cancer patient described earlier, he told himself (when in a state of relaxed concentration) that he was getting healthier and healthier. He soon began to benefit from this approach.

Next, John was taught bridging exercises and developed his other channels. As a result, he was able to use all five channels during his mental healing sessions.

Then he pictured himself drinking a glass of medicine that tasted and smelled like he imagined a strong medicine would. It felt cool and slippery going down his throat. Then he imagined this medicine reaching his colon and coating it with a soothing balm. As he told himself his colon was healing, he felt a deep calmness spread within his bowels.

With these exercises, John achieved a significant easing of his symptoms and a marked increase in his ability to handle stress. To avoid a reoccurence of his illness, he continued daily practice of this image and other soothing and calming images, even after his symptoms were gone.

John became cheerful again and he was able to resume his active and vigorous lifestyle. He was able to work a full day at his business and come home with enough energy to enjoy being a husband and father.

Another patient also had a strong auditory-verbal channel that she used in an interesting way. Like a cheerleader cheering her team to victory, she mentally cheered on her medicine to defeat her stubborn case of tuberculosis. Her results were excellent.

Of course, all of these patients used conventional medical treatment at the same time they practiced self-guided imagery.

HOW TO USE TRIGGERS TO MAKE MENTAL HEALING EVEN MORE POWERFUL

Another way to increase the power of mental healing is to use triggers. In addition to using multiple channels, before ending a session these patients made a trigger. Later, whenever they fired this trigger, it created a condensed version of the entire mental healing session—a "mini-session." They fired it when they had a few spare moments, such as when taking a shower or waiting for a red light to change. Those "wasted" moments were put to good use. It was a time-saving way to get in extra practice.

THREE STEPS FOR USING CHANNEL POWER AND TRIGGERS TO HELP YOU HEAL YOUR BODY

1. Imagine (in as many channels as you can) your illness being cured. Although this image can be other than a picture, preferably it will include your seeing channel.
2. Make this image as literal or as fanciful as you choose. What matters is that it is an image that seems right for you. This indicates that the images come from your unconscious mind —and your unconscious mind is exactly what you are trying to communicate with.
3. Set aside at least thirty minutes a day for a full multichannel imagery healing session. Practice making triggers at each session and fire them at various times throughout the day.

Caution: Never use mental healing in place of regular medical treatment. After all, you want results. A coach would not get his team all fired up to win the big game and then not use his first string quarterback. Nor would a dressmaker buy the best design she could and then not buy any thread with which to sew the dress together. You will need to continue with your checkups, go to the dentist when your tooth aches, give yourself first aid when you injure yourself, and consult a physician for serious symptoms.

Yet, you can expect this improved method of multichannel mental healing to increase significantly your chances of recovery, besides making the treatment process more comfortable.

CHANNEL POWER TECHNIQUES TO HELP YOU PREVENT ILLNESS

In addition to using these imagery techniques for combatting specific illnesses, you can use them to help prevent illness.

A small revolution is going on in medical practice. More emphasis is being placed on maintaining health and preventing illness, instead of the expensive and often desperate attempt to treat illness once established. This trend toward prevention has been heralded as "the wave of the future," and a more intelligent way to attack health problems.

There is considerable evidence that daily imagery sessions help prevent illness and promote continuing good health and longevity. Studies have shown that mental imagery can lower blood pressure, change heart rate, regulate blood flow and effect body chemistry.

For example, one research project demonstrated the amazing power of imagination on body chemistry. The researchers found that their subjects, who had a food allergy, could eat food that they usually were allergic to and have *no* allergic reaction. The researchers were able to do this by having their subjects imagine that they were eating nonallergic foods.

Another study found that mental imagery actually increased the number of cancer-fighting lymphocytes in the blood of healthy people. Conversely, negative thoughts decreased the blood's germ-fighting cells.

Stress—such as death of a loved one, divorce, financial difficulties, and trouble with your boss—also has been found to impair your disease-fighting immune system.

Due to the profound effect imagery has on our bodies, mental imagery is taught at stress management courses, which are designed to help prevent illness. Most participants with hypertension are able to reduce their blood pressure, and some no longer need medication. Other illnesses are also helped.

These courses are a key part of prevention programs at such hospitals and medical centers as the Preventive Medicine Institute at the Georgia Baptist Hospital in Atlanta, and the S. W. Richardson Institute for Preventive Medicine at the Methodist Hospital in Houston.

These programs recommend daily imagery sessions. Like preventing major problems with a storage battery by frequently recharging it before it goes dead, drawing off the toxic effects of too much stress and building up your body's health-promoting defenses will avoid major problems from developing in your body.

Such imagery doesn't have to be about illness or health if you are already healthy. It need not even be goal-directed. Eliminating negative thoughts will promote health. However, simply stopping a thought is not possible because some kind of thought always occupies our minds. A positive or neutral thought is needed to fill the space held by the negative one. There is a study that shows that simply relaxing and thinking of the number "one" over and over produces relief from psychosomatic illness, lowering blood pressure and removing other signs of stress.

There is a large body of research showing that meditation also does this. Instead of the word *one*, a mantra is silently repeated. A mantra is a word that has no meaning, such as "Um." It is supposed to be especially chosen to meet the mystic needs of the meditator. But you will notice that the word *one* has been shown to work as well. Apparently, any neutral word will do.

However, instead of using only your hearing channel, you can use more channels and imagine a pleasant scene if you prefer.

HEALTH-PROMOTING IMAGERY: THE MOST POWERFUL TECHNIQUES FOR AVOIDING ILLNESS AND PROMOTING GOOD HEALTH

The most powerful way to use imagery techniques for avoiding illness and promoting robust good health is to use the same secrets that work for Mental Healing Imagery. These techniques bear repeating here: have a clear target, use all five channels, head off problems by practicing daily, use triggers for mini-sessions, and imagine while in a state of relaxed attention or while self-hypnotized. The systematic use of these techniques is called Health Promoting Imagery.

We have already learned, both from the work with athletes and with cancer patients, that end-result imagery is extremely powerful. Although I have discussed research that shows imagining neutral or pleasant images reduces stress and helps prevent illness, goal-directed imagery is even more effective. Some researchers believe that this technique is the most powerful one of all. Have a clear target.

Likewise, we have seen how multichannel thinking is far more potent than single-channel thinking. If needed, develop all of your channels with bridging exercises and use as many channels as you can, preferably all five.

Daily practice will lessen the effects of stress. Stress has been shown to accumulate and, when it becomes too much, it is "the straw that breaks the camel's back," causing illness. You have, undoubtedly, experienced how much more difficult it is to cope when several misfortunes happen close together. Not only does it feel worse, but this is the time sickness usually strikes. Health-Promoting Imagery sessions, practiced daily, will drain off the effects of stress and help prevent it from accumulating.

What has been said about using triggers for mental healing mini-sessions also holds true for Health-Promoting Imagery. You can have much of the benefit of a full session in a brief time. It's surprising how firing your trigger at odd moments throughout the day will relax you quickly and deeply.

Finally, imagining a full session when in a state of relaxed concentration seems to be more effective than doing mental imagery when in your ordinary state of consciousness. Set aside about twenty minutes a day where you are unlikely to be interrupted. Relax, concentrate, and use one of those exercises. My own personal experience is that using these techniques when hypnotized adds further to their effectiveness. A further chapter will explain fully how you can use these methods with self-hypnosis, if you like.

A most welcome extra benefit of practicing these exercises daily is that you will have more energy and be more alert throughout the day. Your mind will be sharper and faster, so you will be able to think on your feet better. Situations that used to stress you will bother you less or even no longer bother you.

HOW ALICE USED HEALTH-PROMOTING IMAGERY TO AVOID "BURNOUT" FROM A HIGH-STRESS JOB

Alice used her Health-Promoting Imagery after she consulted me about her constant fatigue. "I must be suffering from burnout," she told me. She had a demanding job as a social worker for the court. Her job was to protect children from being neglected or otherwise abused. Dealing with angry parents around such important—sometimes life-and-death—issues was highly stressful.

She had always been healthy and full of energy, but now, in addition to being tired all the time, she had frequent bouts of indigestion and insomnia. Sometimes, her blood pressure readings at the doctor's office were too high. Alice was still young—in her early thirties—but she felt old.

I taught her how to use Health-Promoting Imagery. When I instructed her to imagine, in all five channels, how she wanted to feel, she confided, "I want to be energetic again, with a spring in my step, a smile on my face. My voice should be calm and low pitched. I've been told I have a deep sultry voice, kind of sexy. Now, I often sound high-pitched and strident. I want to feel light instead of heavy." She paused a moment and then continued, "I guess I want to smell fresh and clean, but I have no idea how I want to taste," and burst out laughing. This four-channel image was her target.

Her feeling channel was excellent, but she needed to increase her other channels. She accomplished this rapidly with the bridging exercises and was able to imagine her target clearly in four channels.

Then, each afternoon around five, she would relax for twenty to thirty minutes in a reclining chair, close her eyes, and imagine all the tension in her body draining out and leaving her softly relaxed. Then, she mentally saw herself walking in the country on a sunny summer day. The air smelled fresh. Her step had a spring to it. Her face was smiling, and she felt as if she was walking on a cloud, full of energy. Alice admired how healthy she looked and felt.

She then involved her taste and smell channels by imagining herself drinking an aromatic health-giving potion.

Another image she used was taking a luxurious bubble bath full of silky, fragrant rose petals that caressed her body as they floated by.

Alice also imagined herself talking in her naturally low pitched manner to friends. Then she imagined keeping herself calm and speaking in a low key when confronting parents who had abused their children.

Throughout the day, she would have mini-sessions. She would fire the triggers she had made during her Health-Promoting Imagery sessions. When she fired those triggers, Alice would recapture those good feelings she had when she was practicing her full sessions and feel much calmer.

After just a few days of practicing her Health-Promoting Imagery sessions, she was surprised that her responses to difficult situations were much better. She didn't get upset as easily. Alice could listen to her supervisor criticize how she handled a case, take the suggestions she, Alice, believed were useful, and feel good about herself. When a frustrated mother screamed at her, Alice didn't get as anxious as she used to and calmed down in a short time after the confrontation.

Her doctor was pleased that he was getting consistent normal blood pressure readings now. Her digestion was good and she slept well.

"Best of all," she exclaimed when she reported to me, "I have enough pep at the end of a day to go out and have a good time."

FIVE STEPS FOR HEALTH-PROMOTING IMAGERY SESSIONS

1. Have a clear target.
2. Imagine with five channels.
3. Practice twenty minutes a day.
4. Create triggers and use them for mini-sessions.
5. Imagine in a state of relaxed concentration.

*HEALTH-PROMOTING IMAGERY HELPS YOU GET MORE
OUT OF LIFE AND LIVE LONGER*

It is self-evident that the healthier you are, the more you are apt to get out of life and the longer you are likely to live. Dr. K. R. Pelleton, of the University of California School of Medicine, has researched the effects on mental imagery techniques on promoting long life. The author of many books, including *Longevity: Fulfilling Our Biological Potential,* he finds that these imagery techniques hold great promise for increasing the quality and length of your life span.

The refinements in the science of imagery, described in this chapter, make mental imagery a powerful tool to help you maintain or regain your health. Practice using these specific techniques. Although easy to do, they need to be done correctly to be effective. Many people who did not have success with the older, less exact imagery methods will find these improvements are "just what the doctor ordered."

7

Gain New Relief from Emotional Pain by Using the Triple Split Technique

The same powerful trigger and multichannel techniques that you can use to help relieve physical pain can also be adapted and used to relieve—and even *erase*—emotional pain.

People suffer emotional pain for a variety of reasons: the loss of loved ones, mistreatment as children, life-threatening traumas such as combat, accidents, fire, earthquakes, storms, floods, or the debilitating effects of disease. Even when the event is long over, victims often are haunted by powerful memories.

Soldiers, who many years ago experienced war's death and destruction, can have unrelenting, ongoing nightmares today. Some people grieve the death of a spouse overly long—sometimes forever—depriving themselves of the opportunity for new relationships (and suffering severe depression, which is bad for their physical health). Rape victims sometimes remain excessively fearful for extreme lengths of time, restricting their social life and movements.

All trauma victims, such as those just mentioned, may suffer a variety of problems. These may include all or some of the following: poor concentration, difficulty working, trouble enjoying loved ones and other people, depression, anxiety, insomnia, and fiendish nightmares.

It's bad enough having to go through the original suffering of a painful experience, but continuing to feel old pain is pointless. Yet, many of us do not know how to get over past hurts and find them to be insurmountable obstacles to happiness.

Over the years, as I keep learning new methods, providing help to people with such problems has become increasingly easy. Psychoanalytically oriented therapy with its endless talking and teasing out transference behaviors was effective but slow. Transactional Analysis combined with Gestalt therapy enabled me to move clients quickly to the original roots of their problem.

One difficulty remained, however. These later methods relied on patients having an abreaction—reliving the original emotional pain, as described in Chapter 2. Although the results are worth it, it is too much like performing surgery without an anesthetic. People are frightened of undergoing an abreaction and some avoid getting the help they need. Others cannot tolerate reliving the past and become physically sick.

Fortunately, new psychological methods have provided a way to greatly ease and even eliminate mental anguish without having to relive the emotional pain. This is done with the *Triple Split* technique, which is based on the principle of *dissociation.*

Dissociation is the ability to separate yourself from some event. The detachment you used when you viewed yourself (in the preceding chapters) from the viewpoint of a movie director directing yourself as an actor is a form of dissociation. Dissociation creates a split between your emotions and your memories—those memories no longer pain you.

In addition, clinical experience has shown that the more you are dissociated, the more effectively are your emotions split off from ordinarily painful memories. And once this emotional split is made, it continues to permanently insulate you from such antiquated and useless pain.

I remember one patient in particular with whom I used this technique to excellent advantage. (We will call him Alex.) He presented an interesting therapeutic challenge.

HOW A FORMER PRISONER OF WAR INSULATED HIMSELF FROM HIS OLD EMOTIONAL PAIN

Alex had suffered terribly when he was a Japanese prisoner of war. His health deteriorated from the starvation and physical abuse he endured from his captors. While he was imprisoned, he caught and ate insects to stay alive. In spite of his revulsion, it enabled him to survive until he was liberated to be with his family once more. Now, thirty years later, he suffered from chronic tension and bouts of depression.

When he talked about his POW days, the terrible memories affected him so badly that he became anxious and his blood-sugar level became abnormal, causing him to become physically ill, nauseated, and dizzy.

Our psychiatric team decided that inducing an abreaction as a way of treating him would be too dangerous. It might cause more physical problems than he already had. Even talking about his war experiences made him worse. More importantly, Alex told us he did not want that style of treatment. So pushing him into an abreaction was not an option.

For a while, I handled Alex's treatment by avoiding the root of his problems. Instead, I helped him cope more effectively with his day-to-day problems: disciplining his daughter without feeling guilty, and constructively settling disagreements with his wife. This brought him some relief, but it looked as if he would need constant help to cope with the problems in daily living caused by his underlying problem.

Fortunately, during the course of his treatment, I learned about a new method for helping victims of overwhelming, painful experiences — the Triple Split technique. It seemed made to order for Alex. The treatment did not bring out buried pain, so it would not upset him emotionally or physically, yet it would provide him with the relief he needed. In fact, when I started teaching him bridging exercises to help prepare him for our main work, he benefited greatly from the relaxation these exercises produce. Only after he was able to achieve rapid and complete relaxation and do all the imaginary bridging well did we start using the Triple Split technique. It enabled him to calmly look at those memories that had been so pregnant with pain. He responded excellently. What seemed like an endless case was resolved in just a few months.

HOW TO USE THE TRIPLE SPLIT TECHNIQUE TO REPLACE MENTAL PAIN WITH MENTAL PEACE

Like Alex, you may carry pain inside you from memories of a personal disaster: the death of a loved one, rejection by a lover, divorce, accidental injuries, fires, earthquakes, storms, the horrors of combat, prison camps, childhood abuse, the unspeakable invasion of one's most personal privacy: rape. These, and many more, provide the basis for emotional trauma.

You've probably wondered why some people recover so well from such traumas. How do they form such a tough scar over their injury? Some even gain an added dimension to their personality, seeming wiser and deeper. Yet others carry their trauma like a raw wound, the specter of the past continuing to blight their present lives. They use forgetting as an attempt at solution, but this does not always work. Freud called such forgetting "repression" and found that it broke down when a person is under stress.

A better solution is to change your emotional feeling about the memory—remove the pain. This way you do not have to spend energy on keeping the memory out of awareness. Also, you have at your conscious disposal the lessons that are in that experience.

Linda, who was raped when she was fifteen, was still troubled, at twenty-four, by the memory of her experience. Although she never forgot it, she avoided not only thinking about it, but also anything that might remind her of what had happened. You would be surprised at how many things can trigger a memory. She also developed a fear of closeness with any man.

Obviously, this wholesale system of avoiding all men as a way of protecting herself cramped her lifestyle. After I treated her with the Triple Split method, she was able to look at her rape much more calmly and objectively. This enabled her to make the fine distinctions we all need to make about whom and when to trust. Eventually, she met and married a warm and caring man.

You can use this marvelous method to free yourself from the effects of upsetting experiences in your past that might be still affecting you, causing you to feel sad, depressed, irritable, or anxious.

Since abreactions are avoided rather than encouraged, a therapist is not usually needed. You can do it yourself. However, the method will work best if you are already adept at doing the exercises from the preceding chapters (especially those in Chapter 4), which are designed to expand your mind. It is strongly recommended that you become proficient at these exercises before using the Triple Split method.

THE TRIPLE SPLIT TECHNIQUE: STEP BY STEP

1. Begin by relaxing and imagining a tranquil and enjoyable experience. Use bridging techniques as you do this. When you feel relaxed and as peaceful as you can, create a trigger for it. You can use this trigger to restore these feelings whenever you think you might need them to remain calm during the whole procedure.

2. Now, imagine the part of you that observes and analyzes situations and people. Most of us enjoy "people watching." That is the state you want. Float the Observer outside yourself so it can watch and observe along with you.

   Try to have your Observer see how calm you look and how your chest rises and falls with each breath. If you can do this, it will make the procedure even more effective. But the method works well without it, so if you cannot imaging this, simply go ahead with the following steps, anyway.

3. On the far wall, just as if you were watching a movie of yourself, project the upsetting past episode from which you want relief. (If more than one scene is connected to your pain, save it for another Triple Split session.) Keeping yourself calm and separated from the unpleasant scene, have your Observer watch and learn (on a conscious and unconscious level) the lessons in that past incident along with you. Take all the time you need. The nature of the unconscious mind is such that it can condense time and learn almost instantly.

4. When you have completed step 3, be sure to thank your past self for helping you and showing you what happened. It is important to respect and appreciate your unconscious mind. Explain to your past self that you are its future self and you will protect and take care of it.

5. Float this past self back into your heart and give it big hug, allowing yourself to really enjoy it. Again, take your time. When you are done, float your Observer back in, so you are all together.

6. Finally, imagine yourself in the future, behaving in new ways as a result of your new feelings and outlook. Notice how little things no longer upset you, your concentration is better, you are more patient, it is easier for you to love a greater range of people, and your zest for living returns. Open your eyes and enjoy your new found sense of peace.

If you have more than one bad memory, repeat this process for each one. You may prefer to do this on different days, instead of trying to do it all at once.

Here is an outline of the main steps for using this marvelous Triple Split method. In this technique, your real self calmly directs the event, your Observer watches along with you, and your past self endures the upsetting experience. This makes for a powerfully effective dissociated state that will keep you relaxed and calm, and will allow only your imagined self from the past to have any painful emotion.

Six-Step Outline of the Triple Split Technique

1. Relax and imagine a calm and peaceful scene.
2. Imagine the Observer at your side.
3. On a distant screen or stage, watch and listen to your past self going through that upsetting experience. Keep yourself calm and separate from your past self.
4. Thank your past self and promise protection.
5. Give this part a big hug. Really enjoy it and float your Observer back in.
6. Imagine yourself in the future with the new feelings you want.

To end the session, refocus your attention on your surroundings. You will feel refreshed and contented.

HOW SHARON RELIEVED MENTAL ANGUISH WITH THE TRIPLE SPLIT TECHNIQUE

Sharon used the Triple Split technique to dramatically relieve herself of the anguish she felt at being betrayed by her lover of three years. She had forced the bad news out of him about three weeks before she saw me, and had been in torment ever since.

Hoping she was wrong, and not wanting to end the relationship, she had put off asking him about it until she could no longer deny her senses. And besides, he was seeing her less and less — much less than she wanted to see him. Finally, she confronted him with her suspicions.

She told me that, when John admitted that there was another woman, she almost wished she had not asked him. His answer felt as if he had thrust a red hot poker into her heart.

Whenever she recalled that scene, she felt that hot poker in her heart again.

To relieve her pain, Sharon used the Triple Split technique during our session. First, she relaxed by using a bridging exercise that included imagining herself taking a steamy whirlpool bubble bath laced with her favorite scent. The bath soothingly massaged her body and delighted her with its fragrance. This was an especially comforting scene for her.

The next step was to float out her Observer. Since she enjoyed sitting on a bench during her lunch hour, watching people in the park, she used this memory to get in touch with her Observer and floated that part out along side of her self.

Third, she imagined herself and her Observer sitting in the balcony of a plush theater. The curtain was a lovely blue velvet and, when it opened, there on the stage she saw herself with John. From the comfort of her balcony seat, she watched with interest as they acted out that scene where he told her it was all over between them.

Sharon remained calm as she watched. But at one point, she began to feel the hot poker in her heart. She realized this was happening because she was getting into the scene. So she made sure she was separate from the Sharon of the past. After that, the real Sharon was again calm and intrigued by what she saw heard, and got a whole new perspective on what had happened between John and her. After she had watched long enough to feel she had learned all she could from that scene, she drew the certain closed and imagined that her past self — the one who had that exchange with John — stepped out in front of the curtain. Sharon thanked her past self for demonstrating that scene and told her that she was Sharon of the present who would love and protect her. Then she floated her into her heart and enjoyed giving her a big hug.

Finally, she floated in her Observing Adult, so that she was all together. Then she opened her eyes.

She was immensely gratified that she could now think of that same episode without getting upset. After that Triple Split session, she though of her former lover less and less. When she did think of him, she felt more objective about him and could see his good and bad points. The old ache was gone—no more hot poker. Her world started looking brighter. She enjoyed things again and was her usual cheery self.

Soon she was dating again and the next time love came calling, she profited from her experiences with John and chose a man with deeper feelings and commitment. She never had to use the Triple split method again.

Sharon might have joined the ranks of so many who endlessly pine over a lost lover. While not as traumatic as rape or betrayal, broken hearts are one of the most common forms of mental anguish. Some rejected lovers are like walking wounded. Anything can set the wound bleeding again.

Some decide never to risk such a hurt again and forever deny themselves the chance at successful love. Others test out prospective lovers so hard, they drive them away and reduce their own chances for new love to zero.

If you are among the ranks of the unrequited, like trauma victims, you too suffer from remembrances. You think of him or her every time you see, hear, taste, or smell something you shared together.

Those things that used to be triggers of happiness are now reminders of what you have lost: specifically, the chance to enjoy such future pleasures with him again. Your pain is caused by ceaselessly recalling images of him. To think of him in this way is like doing double triggering, but with a painful result instead of a pleasant one. You dilute pleasurable memories with the fresh pain of your disappointment, transforming those enjoyable memories into painful ones. This obsessive recalling of your times together is like rubbing crushed glass into your heart. Obviously, you do not want such an outcome.

"Don't think about him anymore" is good advice but difficult to achieve. I know people who have gone so far as to yell at themselves to stop thinking of their ex-lover. They dig their fingernails painfully into their palms or sharply snap a large rubber band on their wrists, trying to get themselves to stop remembering.

A much easier and effective method is to use another triggering technique. This technique operates on the principle that you cannot think of more than one thing at a time.

This system will also transform those painful emotions to more comfortable ones.

A THREE-STEP TRIGGER FOR MENDING YOUR BROKEN HEART

1. Relax and Create a Trigger for Some Happy Scenes

Relax (you might want to do some of the bridging exercises as a warm up). Imagine some happy and rewarding scenes—which, of course, do not include your lost lover. These may be memories or fantasies. Create a trigger for them.

2. Fire This Trigger When You Think of Him or Her

Then, whenever you find yourself thinking about your former lover, fire your trigger and you will automatically start thinking of these positive scenes instead.

You will accomplish two things with this method: first, you will eventually stop thinking about him or her and, second, you will be diluting your painful feelings so that you can think of this person and remain comfortable.

3. Persist Until the Obsession Ends

Just before you achieve this breakthrough, you will suddenly find yourself deluged with these troublesome thoughts, as if the method was suddenly failing. Be certain to persist because, for reasons we do not understand, this happens just before the dying of most habits. It is as if the obsession was making a final effort to survive and is throwing all of its reserve power into one final win-or-lose battle. However, if you persist and continue to trigger substitute images, the obsessive thinking will decrease dramatically at this point.

The pleasant thoughts you trigger, as a substitute for thoughts of him or her, will desensitize your pain, like the way the system for curing phobias desensitizes your fear.

HOW KAREN USED TRIGGERS TO GET OVER HER LOST LOVE AND GET ON WITH HER LIFE

Karen was one of my clients who used this double trigger technique to rid herself of this type of problem.

First, she relaxed herself and vividly recalled the time she graduated from high school. Her favorite aunt had been intensely proud of her. She visualized Aunt Sue's face in detail and heard her words of warm approval and admiration. Karen was especially gratified by the tone of her aunt's voice. When Karen was feeling this fully, she grasped her right thumb to create a trigger for that memory.

In the same way, she also created a trigger for the enjoyment she feels when playing a good game of tennis. Thus whenever she grasped her thumb, she would automatically think about both these things and the good feelings that go with them.

Lastly, she practiced in her imagination. She thought of her lover and then grasped her thumb. Automatically, her mind shifted to thinking of those happy memories, easing her pain.

After this, whenever she thought of him, she would fire her trigger. It worked well for three days, and she thought of him less and less. But, on the fourth day, it seemed he entered her mind more than ever. Although she felt discouraged and wanted to give up, she remembered my warning that this would happen. She persisted with the double triggering operation and by the end of the day, she rarely thought of him. She was free!

HOW TO USE THE TRIPLE SPLIT TECHNIQUE TO RELIEVE ANXIETY, GET A CLEARER OUTLOOK, AND FIND SOLUTIONS

The Triple Split technique not only can be used for recovering from past hurts, but also for getting relief from a current upsetting situation. Although anxiety can be a helpful spur to action, too much anxiety clouds your thinking and interferes with finding effective solutions. However, if you use the Triple Split method, you will be able to contemplate the situation calmly, without anxiety, and think about it more clearly. You will get a new perspective on it and new solutions will present themselves to you.

HOW EMILE USED THE TRIPLE SPLIT TECHNIQUE TO SOLVE A VEXING FAMILY AND BUSINESS PROBLEM

Emile had some tough decisions to made: He owned an electronics company and was so successful that he wanted to expand. To get more capital invested into his company, he had to reorganize and take in a new partner. Also, a section of his company was not productive and there was the possibility that he might have to eliminate it. But his uncle, Dan, was heading that section, and Emile didn't know what to do with him. His uncle had helped raise him after Emile's father died. Also, Dan had introduced him to his wife and she adored his uncle. Emile was just too close to the situation.

He was worried about the expansion of his business, the need for more money and increased overhead expenses, the new partner, and being fair to all of his employees, including his uncle.

"I just can't seem to think straight," he told me. "I used to talk things over with my wife and my uncle. But, this time, my wife is emotionally involved because of her feelings for Uncle Dan. And, of course, Dan is directly involved and I can't expect him to be objective about himself."

Although I was not an expert on business, I knew how to use the mind. I taught Emile the Triple Split method. It would literally give him some distance from his problem and enable him to look at things in a detached manner.

Emile projected the situation on an imaginary stage and had discussions with the partner, Dan, and his wife. Then, like a playwright and director, he had them try out different roles and jobs. One thing he realized as he did this was that he was too anxious to have the partner come in for his money. Also, the partner did not seem to like his uncle, Dan.

"It came to me in a flash," he told me later, as he described his Triple Split session. "I was too eager to please that prospective partner. His attitude toward Dan would be a constant irritant. Dan is good at what he does and I can use him in the head office. I decided not to be frightened of losing that partner and I talked it over with him. He agreed to invest money, but not be active in the running of the business. What a relief."

The reorganization went smoothly and whenever Emile needed a cool head to think through a problem, he used the Triple Split method.

HOW CONNIE USED THE TRIPLE SPLIT METHOD TO MAKE AN IMPORTANT DECISION

Connie used this technique to solve her anxiety about whether to marry. She had been devastated by her divorce from her first husband three years ago. With her children grown and no job skills, she was suddenly alone and on her own after having been a housewife for twenty years.

She had to get used to living by herself, earning her own living and being completely independent. She managed to get a job as a timekeeper at a hospital. Officially, the job was part time, but she usually worked thirty-nine hours — almost a full-time schedule. She managed to rebuild her life and eventually met Carl. They fell in love and planned to marry. Then he was transferred to a city two hundred miles away.

Carl started to put pressure on Connie to marry him and move to his city. But she became worried and anxious. It would mean giving up her friends here and leaving her job. With her seniority, she had a chance of being put on full-time at her present job. This would give her higher wages and paid vacation and sick time. She hated to give that up. Furthermore, it would use up most of her savings to buy a condominium for them to live in. She was torn.

After she used the Triple Split technique, Connie told me, "I clearly saw how I would become just as dependent on Carl as I had been on my first husband. Look where that left me. I never want to be that vulnerable again.

"I told Carl," she went on, "that instead of setting a 'calendar date' for the wedding, I'm willing to set a 'situation date.' This means that when I can achieve the same things to keep my independence in his city—if I found as good or better a job there and could keep my savings—I would marry him. Or if he found a way to move back to my city, I would marry him."

When I saw her a three months later, she was still looking for a job in his city and he was trying to get transferred back to hers. But most importantly, Connie felt good about her decision.

"It's hard having a love life that spans two cities. But it's better than being worried sick and frightened about the future. I did get put on full time at work. It sure helped to get a clear picture of things," she said.

8

Mental Tapes: How To Erase Negative Messages and Open the Way to Your Full Potential

Besides the powerful influence of conscious images, you can be profoundly influenced by unconscious images. Messages can be given directly to our unconscious mind so we are not aware of them. These can be positive messages that help us live a fuller life or they can be negative ones that are destructive and lead to self-defeating behavior.

THE POWER OF NEGATIVE MESSAGES

Sometimes, such messages are given to surgical patients who overhear comments of the staff when under general anesthesia and, supposedly, totally unconscious.

An example of the power of a negative message concerned a man who was unaccountably depressed after a successful operation. He felt hopeless and certain he was going to die. He wept frequently.

110

The medical staff was unable to account for his reaction. He would reject any reassurance of his true medical state, which was excellent. Discussions with him about why he felt this way shed no light on the mystery.

Finally, a startling discovery was made. The patient was hypnotized and then recounted that, when he was completely anesthetized, someone had remarked, "Poor guy. Doesn't have a chance. He'll never make it." This served as a death verdict to our patient's unconscious mind and was the cause of his depressed attitude. Yet, like anyone under anesthesia, consciously he had not been able to recall a word.

The hypnotist was puzzled. There was no reason for anyone to make such a pronouncement about this patient. His surgery had gone smoothly and there was no evidence of tumors or malignancy.

The possibility that the words were part of the patient's imagination (perhaps he had a dream) was considered. But when the surgical team was told about the patient's remarks, the chief surgeon exclaimed, "My God! I made those remarks to the nurse about a discussion we were having just before entering the O.R. We were talking about the chances of my neighbor's son getting into med school. I meant my neighbor's son didn't have a chance."

No one had believed a patient who is unconscious from anesthesia (or from anything else, for that matter) could hear what is going on. The possibility of influencing the patient under these conditions had not even been thought of.

When the facts were thoroughly explained to the patient, he still resisted believing them until the surgeon himself explained his remarks and what he had really meant by them. At that point, the patient's mood dramatically lifted and he recovered from his depression.

It is now the policy of that hospital (and several others) not only to refrain from negative comments during surgery but to also take advantage of the suggestibility of an anesthetized patient and make positive comments and suggestions about healing quickly and comfortably. Such positive suggestions do indeed make for easier and speedier recovery after surgery. Patients, in one study, who were given positive suggestions while being operated on, were able to be discharged, on the average, 2.42 days earlier than a matched group who were not given such influence.

HOW WE GET MOST OF OUR NEGATIVE MESSAGES

Most of us are influenced by childhood messages we have long forgotten but which are still active in our unconscious.

Eric Berne, psychiatrist and founder of Transactional Analysis, was intrigued by patients who made the same mistakes over and over again in living. It seemed as if their life, like a fairy tale, was already laid out for them by some evil genius who had written a script that they had to follow as if they were under his spell.

Careful investigation of many patients uncovered that something like that was indeed happening. However, it was no fairy tale at work, but the images (sometimes distorted) of childhood. These early images influenced the adult person similarly to the way the overheard comments influenced our surgical patient. However, these early messages could be remembered more easily than any that might be given to an anesthetized patient.

These childhood images influenced important things such as whom and how they loved, how they handled authority, what they thought of themselves, and how they treated themselves and others. These images were able to exert a strong influence on their present daily lives.

For example, Sam could remember frequent admonitions, from loving but frightened parents, to be careful. "Don't cross the street." "Don't go out after dark." "Don't talk to strangers." And on and on, all through his growing years. He had images of not only their words, but of their worried faces and his own fear. Although the images of those voices and faces grew dim, the habitual cautious behavior and fear remained. Sam was an extremely careful and tense man. He spent so much time considering if a woman was safe ("Would she be faithful, would his friends approve, would she be a good mother?") that the women all lost patience and he never married. Countless hours and enormous amounts of energy were spent in avoiding danger of all sorts. Indeed, he was under a spell, but not the spell of a wicked witch, but a spell created by his own mental images. These images were imprinted in all his channels.

In contrast to Sam's messages given to him by a doting overprotective mother, Donna was raised by a disinterested mother who suffered from severe depressive episodes during Donna's early childhood. As a result, Donna's mother would withdraw and ignore her for long hours, performing only the minimal duties to keep her alive. Donna got the message that she wasn't worth much and shouldn't even be around.

Donna grew up with low self-esteem. At times, she felt depressed and suicidal. She let men exploit her. One man lived with her a while and then borrowed her credit card to take a vacation. He ran her debts up to thousands of dollars before she finally revoked her card.

Children, who are frequently told "to be seen and not heard," are being given the message not to be important. Others, who see their parents handle stress with explosive anger, are being taught to handle stress in the same way. Some children are influenced not to feel good about being a girl or boy by parents who clearly show a preference for a different sex.

Insisting that a child always be clean, neat, quiet, considerate and courteous is telling her not to have a childhood. Conversely, encouraging a child to be self-indulgent and giving him no responsibility is telling him not to grow up.

Children abandoned by desertion or death get a message not to be close. If they accept this message, they grow up having shallow love relationships. They are distant and reserved, avoiding intimacy. Often they never marry.

INJUNCTIONS: HOW NEGATIVE MESSAGES INFLUENCE YOU TO MAKE THE SAME MISTAKES OVER AND OVER

Not all children accept these messages. But given how much weaker the position of children is compared to their parents', the messages of parents are hard to resist. And once accepted, these messages, which are images of the way they were treated, exert a powerful hidden influence on their adult lives. This leads to the repetitive self-defeating behavior observed by Berne.

Berne called these early influences "injunctions." Therapists also refer to them as "messages" and "tape loops." They liken them to tape recordings made into endless loops that play the same message over and over again, persistently influencing a person's life.

Injunctions are delivered in various ways that are not readily apparent to the untrained observer. For example, Sam's parents never told him, "Be scared and over-cautious." Indeed they would have been appalled if anyone had recommended that they do so. But they were tense and worried people who did not want any harm to come to their son, and they conveyed the injunction by the way they looked, talked, and treated him. (These hidden or, as Berne called them, ulterior messages are the subject of his best-selling book *Games People Play*).

Donna's mother had severe problems of her own and was just trying to make it through the day. She had no intention of giving her daughter negative messages.

The father, who insists upon his son being "a little gentleman," thinks he is training his son to have character, and is surprised when his son grows up to be dull, stiff, and unable to appreciate life and have fun.

These injunctions can be lost to our conscious mind. We can have forgotten them, and yet their effects remain potent—just as the unfortunate remarks made by the surgeon near his patient, in the case described earlier.

HOW TO "ERASE" NEGATIVE MENTAL TAPES

One way to deal with injunctions is to gain conscious awareness of them. This will enable you to change your beliefs and to behave in ways that are consistent with the new beliefs.

The surgical patient was first made aware of the messages, but then had to be convinced of the truth. He had to change what he believed and decide he was not seriously ill.

Just before the patient made his redecision, his therapist remarked, "And now that you know the truth, you can feel secure and happy again." This positive message, "feel secure and happy," is called a "permission" and is the opposite of a negative message, the "injunction." The timing of permissions is important. The therapist made it just as he saw that the patient finally understood and believed that the root of his problem was his surgeon's chance remarks.

It was also possible for the patient to come spontaneously to the same conclusion unaided, but making the permission explicit ensured that the patient would come to the right conclusion.

RIDDING YOURSELF OF SELF-DEFEATING MESSAGES

The method used to free the surgical patient of his injunction—identifying the injunction, making it conscious, and replacing it with a permission—is similar to how many therapists help people get rid of their self-defeating messages. Childhood memories are vividly recalled, clarifying how the injunctions were given, and the clients can then change their original decision. In place of the negative message, they give themselves a new permission. This process is called making a *redecision.*

This sounds complicated, and I used to think people could only rid themselves of injunctions with the help of a well trained professional. However, when I started teaching clients how to do it themselves, most of them got excellent results using this Redecision Technique on their own.

As you will see, one woman exchanged an injunction that said "Respect your betters" for a permission to respect herself. Another woman rid herself of an injunction that had led her into a pattern of choosing men who exploited her. Many other self-defeating lifestyles have been changed into self-enhancing ones.

THE REDECISION TECHNIQUE FOR OVERCOMING SELF-DEFEATING BEHAVIOR

You can root out your self-defeating messages using the Redecision Technique. Four principles are involved:

1. Recall the early messages
2. Refute your early decision to accept these injunctions and
3. Make a new decision to give yourself new Permissions.
4. Offer protection to your anxious part

The adults—most usually your parents—who urged injunctions on you were powerful and frightening figures to you when you were a child. Of course, they are only images in your mind now, but influencing you as if they were still powerful realities. To counteract their influence, you need to assure your Child ego state that you will protect it from these frightening people.

To begin the Redecision Technique, relax and recall the last time you engaged in the self-defeating behavior you want to change. As you remember this vividly in your visual and auditory channels, you will experience the feelings that attended that behavior. Make a trigger for this. Now, when you press this trigger, it will evoke those same feelings.

Fire your trigger and as you experience those feelings, see an earlier scene during which you had those same feelings. (You will recall, from earlier chapters, this is called "bridging.")

Continue to press this trigger, and recall still earlier times when you had the same feeling until you come to what seems like the first (or a very early) time you experienced these feelings.

You will be imagining the scene in which you were given your injunctions — the wrong messages which run counter to the permissions you want yourself to have. Keep yourself calm and dissociated. See and hear your younger self in that scene out in front of you.

Shelly did this and recalled an early scene in her life where her father spanked her severely as he said, "Now, remember to respect your betters." This had the effect of making Shelly a good little girl, but a shy and unhappy adult. People liked her all right, but she didn't know how to respect herself and stand up for her rights.

Now that she realized the cause of her attitude and behavior, she decided she no longer had to agree with that injunction to "respect her betters." There were no betters, she was as good as anyone else. She lovingly explained this to the mental image of herself as a little girl and gave her permission to feel as important as anyone else. "I'll protect and take care of you. Daddy can't hit you anymore." When Shelly's imaginary little girl believed her, they embraced to seal their new pact.

Next she imagined herself behaving towards others with her new self-respecting attitude. She created a trigger for this new state and, as soon as she could, put her new conviction into practice in the real world.

Shelly began to insist quietly but firmly on respect for her rights. For instance, she no longer allowed herself to be given the less desirable vacation times at work. She insisted the less seniority people defer to her wishes. When she came home from a day's work, her working husband could cook every other day or take her out. Her husband resisted at first, but he was a reasonable man and soon saw the justice of the arrangement. But Shelly had to have a long talk with him first.

Some of her friends were not so reasonable. They had gotten used to Shelly catering to their wishes. They became incensed. "Their friendship isn't worth the cost to my self-esteem," Shelly told me. However, her true friends admired the change and respected her for it. Others were confused by the change, but adapted to it and continued to be her friends.

Her new way of acting made her much more effective at the store where she worked and she was promoted to assistant manager. "But, more important than anything," she confided to me, "I feel really good about myself."

NINE STEPS FOR ELIMINATING SELF-DEFEATING BEHAVIOR

Here are the nine steps of the Redecision Technique for rooting out injunctions and replacing them with new permissions to eliminate self-defeating behavior.

1. Identify your problem behavior you want to change and imagine yourself experiencing that behavior (as the actor not as an on-looker).
2. Become aware of the emotions you are feeling as you perform this behavior. This engages your feeling channel.
3. Keep that feeling and bridge to the earliest time you felt this same way. Using your visual and hearing channel, let that scene unfold in front of you. See your younger self (Child ego state) in the picture.
4. Look and listen for the negative messages (injunctions) your Child is receiving.
5. Redecide to think and feel differently and give your Child permission to think and feel this new way.
6. Make a second trigger for your new permissions.
7. Promise protection and float in your Child and give it a big hug and celebrate your new freedom.
8. Imagine yourself in the future behaving in new and satisfying ways because of your new attitude.

9. Awaken yourself and put this in practice in the real world as soon as possible. Whenever you feel you need your new permission, fire your trigger.

Here is how another woman used this technique to make profound changes in her life.

HOW DONNA USED THE REDECISION TECHNIQUE TO STOP DATING "USERS WHO WERE LOSERS"

Donna, the young woman mentioned earlier who was raised by a depressed mother, used the Redecision Technique to overcome self-defeating messages that were ruining her life. "All the men I get involved with are users who are losers," she confided.

Donna wanted to stop having relationships with men who used her. "They con me out of all my money. They live good for a while but always wind up broke and out of work. One of them got thrown out of school, and another was arrested for stealing a car. I just keep getting the wrong kind of guys—losers. I just don't feel good enough for the other kind. You know, guys that have something on the ball," she told me.

Here is how she went through the Redecision Technique, step by step, to end her self-defeating behavior.

1. Imagine Doing the Problem Behavior

Donna relaxed in her reclining chair and imagined her last boyfriend and how she let him talk her into using her credit card to go on a "vacation" after he had lost his job. She imagined that it was really happening all over again (not as an observer).

2. Become Aware of the Emotions You Are Feeling

As she experienced the painful feelings of that event, she made a trigger by pressing her left leg.

3. Bridge to an Earlier Image

She fired her trigger and, from that feeling channel that was evoked, bridged to seeing and hearing herself in an earlier scene. She saw herself with a previous boyfriend, who lived with her for months, claiming to be looking for work, but who was really spending his time partying and spending all of her money.

She fired her trigger again and saw a time when she cleaned up a sorority clubhouse but wasn't allowed to join.

Finally, Donna saw the earliest image she could remember: she saw herself around the age of five. Mother was in her room with the shades drawn, ignoring everything, including little Donna. Donna's nickname then was "Dee."

(It is okay to go directly to your earliest memory without any intervening ones bridging into awareness.)

4. Look and Listen to the Injunctions

Donna saw Dee crying and asking for attention. Then Dee brought her mother some cookies and her mother ate them. After they were all eaten, her mother put Dee outside the bedroom door and shut her out. Dee looked heartbroken and Donna asked her what she was feeling. Dee answered, "Nobody loves me, I'm no good."

Here, Donna learned her injunction was to be inferior and she was to give to others and get nothing in return.

5. Make a Redecision and Give Yourself Permission

Donna, with strong love in her heart — her message had to be stronger than her mother's — told Dee that she was a good and sweet little girl. Mother was sick and couldn't help yourself. It had nothing to do with Dee and Dee deserved as much as anybody else. Donna talked to her this way until she saw that Dee believed her.

6. Make a Second Trigger

Donna pressed her other leg to make another trigger for her new decision. She could use her second trigger whenever she felt she needed to reinforce her new attitude. If she felt anxious behaving according to her new permissions, she could fire this trigger. It would help her maintain her new way of treating herself.

7. Promise Protection

Donna told Dee she would take care of her now and see to it that she gets the things she needs. Donna would love her and protect her from users and help her avoid getting hurt. She deserved a fine young man who wanted to care for her. Dee gave a great big smile and they embraced.

8. Mentally Rehearse

Donna mentally rehearsed her target behavior: seeing that her needs were met and feeling she deserved her share of attention, caring, and material things. She heard herself graciously saying "no" to unreasonable requests. She also heard herself asking for favors (something she had rarely done—she used to not even ask for a ride home when she was broke).

9. Practice in Real Life

Donna immediately practiced asking for reasonable favors, saying "no" when she felt like it, and mentally giving Dee a great big hug when she did this. Donna also used her past experience with men to avoid potential users. She could spot them at once now. She dated some men who were considerate. She found they weren't as exciting as the other kind, but she also found them much more satisfying in the long run.

She met a handsome, ambitious young man who was working his way through college. She found him to be considerate and responsible. However, she sometimes didn't feel good enough for him and started doing things for him that she didn't want to do. Her bad feelings about this alerted her. She fired her trigger, had a quick "talk" with little Dee, and reminded her that she was good and deserved to be loved. This stopped the old self-defeating behavior before it developed, and Donna resumed relating to her new boyfriend as an equal again.

THE DIRECT PERMISSION TECHNIQUE FOR OVERCOMING SELF-DEFEATING MESSAGES

The Redecision Technique for removing injunctions is powerful and for years I thought it was the only way to do it. However, I discovered that identifying the specific early injunctions in order to counteract its effects was not always necessary.

I was happily surprised when hundreds of college students, who were taking my human potential courses, obtained excellent results without necessarily understanding the roots of their injunctions. They directly gave themselves new permissions without uncovering the early childhood images which created the self-defeating messages.

I was impressed with how well these students could make profound changes in their lives. I wasn't doing therapy with them, I was simply teaching them about permissions and encouraging them to apply what they were learning to their own lives. I personally know of people who are still benefiting from such work years later.

I had stumbled on another effective method of counteracting self-defeating messages: the *Direct Permission Technique*.

However, my experience has been that the Direct Permission Technique works well for many people but not as well for others. For some reason that is not yet understood, some people get better results with the Direct Permission Technique, and others with the Redecision Technique. Both techniques are given so you can experiment and find which one works best for you.

Much of the work in designing the Direct Permission method was done in my college courses. The basic idea was to overcome self-defeating behavior by directly giving yourself the needed permissions. The principles used were understanding, decision, and practice.

First, the students learned what their human rights were and which ones they were lacking. We discussed basic permissions that we, as humans, need in order to lead fulfilling and complete lives. Some authors, like Emanuel Smith who wrote *When I Say No, I Feel Guilty*, call permissions "human rights." Others refer to them as "allowers." After going over these lists of permissions that had been compiled by these various authors, the students identified the ones they needed. Here is the list of permissions the students used:

IT IS ALL RIGHT FOR ME TO:

Make mistakes
Belong
Go at my own pace
Say what I'm feeling
Decide what is best for me
Do what I decide is best for me
Be human
Finish things
Accomplish
Be here
Be myself
Be young
Be a full adult
Get close
Succeed
Be healthy (well and sane)
Be important
Feel what I feel
Figure things out
Be my own final judge
Not justify my behavior to others
Refuse to solve others' problems
Change my mind
Say, "I don't know"
Be independent of other people's goodwill
Be illogical
Say, "I don't understand"
Say, "I don't care"
Decide about me
Not explain myself to others
Not have to win an argument
Ask for what I want

Say, "No"
Not need you to like me
Have my say

Identifying your rights, giving yourself permission to change, making specific plans on how to change, and practicing the new behavior in your daily life are the basic elements of this system. Students, in my classes, selected the permissions they needed from the list above. Then they decided it was all right for them to behave in ways consistent with those permissions. Third, they planned how to put into practice the new ways they were to act.

After only a few weeks of practicing their new behaviors in the real world, many reported profound changes in their personal and on-the-job relationships.

For instance, one woman gave herself permission to be close to people. She decided she would become friendlier, more involved, and enjoy them. Another man, after he gave himself permission to respect himself and decided it was all right for him to say "no," began to supervise his workers more effectively. "Careful Sam" identified his need to take more risks and be more confident things would work out. He gave himself permission by deciding it would be all right to do this, and made specific plans to practice this new behavior. Whenever he found himself worrying, he would fire a trigger he had created which recalled a beautiful sunset. This had a calming effect on him and took his mind off his worry.

As a result, eventually, the distant woman not only enjoyed many friends, but she also smoothed out a rocky marriage which brought her great joy. The supervisor who learned to say "no" was promoted. And careful Sam took a chance and got married.

Two principles need to be kept in mind. First, do not expect sudden and severe changes. It is better to make gradual and steady changes. Second, do not throw out the good with the bad.

For instance, concern about consequences can be a useful thing. Worry can motivate you to find solutions to the problem you are worrying about. You wouldn't want to get rid of such a trait. But Sam overdid it and worried too much. To counteract his injunction, he made a rule that he was not to worry more than ten minutes a day unless his worrying was generating some new solutions.

One thing that is always helpful is the encouragement and praise of fellow classmates, group members, and friends. Since Sam did not have such a group he could call on for support, he imagined being encouraged by people whose opinion he valued. He created a trigger for this and fired it after he acted in his new manner—acting more boldly without worry. Self-praise is probably even more important and Sam was instructed to praise himself frequently for his attempts as well as for his successes.

Also, to help him perform his new behavior in the real world, Sam practiced in his imagination.

To use this Direct Permission Technique, which omits making the early injunctions conscious, follow the outline given below. When selecting those permissions you think you need, you may wish to talk this over with a good friend and then follow this outline.

SEVEN-STEP OUTLINE FOR THE PERMISSION TECHNIQUE

1. Select the permissions you need.
2. Relax yourself and, using at least three channels, imagine that part of you which needs these new rights.
3. Give that part permission and encouragement to think and feel this new way.
4. Promise protection and float that part back into yourself, give it a big hug and celebrate.
5. Mentally rehearse your target. Make a trigger.
6. Imagine getting a lot of approval and support.
7. Put this into practice in the real world as soon as possible. Whenever you feel you need your new permission, fire your trigger.

BILL USES THE DIRECT PERMISSION TECHNIQUE TO DEEPEN HIS ABILITY TO SHOW LOVE

Bill was a young man who was overly controlled. He felt he had to hide his feelings and take care of those he loved whatever the cost. He stood tall and clenched his teeth a lot (funny but true).

When Bill came to see me, he had been divorced for two years. At the time his wife filed for divorce, he was stunned. It had come as a complete surprise to him. A hard worker, he had provided well for his wife and son. They had a nice home, fine clothes, a good school for his son, and two cars.

His wife had told him over the years that he rarely showed affection. She had given up hoping that he would change and had found another man who she felt related to her in a genuine way. "He is open with his feelings and tells me how much he cares. If he's hurt or worried, he lets me know that too," she had told him.

Bill admitted that he found it uncomfortable to tell his wife and son how much he loved them. He would give them things instead. He took an overly protective stance, feeling he shouldn't burden his wife with his troubles. If he was tired from an exhausting day at work and his wife wanted to eat out, he wouldn't tell her he preferred to eat at home, but took her out instead. She never knew about the difficult times when his business almost went bankrupt. She only sensed something was the matter.

However, it went further than being secretive with his family. Bill seldom told anyone how he felt. Once he had walked home three miles instead of asking someone at work to drive out of their way and take him home. He didn't even let anyone know that his car was broken down and was in the repair shop. For some reason, it was important for him to always appear strong and confident.

Although proud of his accomplishments—a college graduate, he was a partner in an accounting firm, president of the local Rotary Club, and the best bowler on his league—Bill felt distant from people and vaguely dissatisfied. When his wife left him, he was devastated.

Now that he had regained his composure, he carefully thought over his ex-wife's complaints and realized that she was right. He was having trouble expressing himself to women he dated. Bill was handsome and was able to date many women, but the only one who stayed interested in him was emotionally constricted herself. Bill found he didn't like that trait in her and finally understood why his wife had left him.

Bill wanted to change and become more human: feel okay when saying what he is feeling, admit he has needs and ask for what he wants. These were the permissions he took from the list given earlier. His target was to instill these permissions into his personality.

Here is a step by step description of how he used the Permission Technique to give himself the new permissions he needed to end his self-defeating behavior.

1. Select the Permissions You Need

Bill chose to give himself two permissions: to be human and get his needs met, and to say what he is feeling. This meant he could ask for emotional support. If he felt like not doing something, he could decline. Also, if he wanted something, he could ask for it. And, of course, he was to feel okay about expressing his feelings.

2. Relax and Imagine the Part of You that Needs These New Rights

Bill relaxed on his couch and got in touch with the part that felt uncomfortable and wanted to change. Then he floated that part out in front of him and imagined it standing in front of him. He saw himself as a little boy trying to act grown up.

3. Give Yourself Permission and Encouragement to Think and Feel This New Way

He held an imaginary conversation with his little boy part. Bill intuitively knew, as no one else knew, what the little boy in him needed to hear, and lovingly told him it was okay to admit he couldn't do everything. It was all right to get help, ask for what he needed and say how he felt.

4. Promise Protection and Give It a Big Hug

When Bill saw his little boy self stop trying to look brave and, instead, relax and smile, he knew the little boy part of him was convinced. Bill promised to protect him, floated him back in and gave him a big hug, celebrating his new freedom.

5. Mentally Rehearse Your Target, Then Make a Trigger

Next, Bill imagined himself in the future behaving in new and satisfying ways because of his new attitude. Using three main channels—seeing, hearing and feeling—he imagined telling close friends how he felt. He also imagined asking for things he needed and taking care of his own needs before somebody else's.

Checking out how he felt in these imaginary situations, Bill felt comfortable with most people. He could tell from whom he would get favorable responses. However, he imagined he would get bad responses from some others. He decided to relate to these people in his old guarded way. Bill could see where his old system worked well in certain business relationships.

When he was imagining himself enjoying being open with his friends, Bill made a trigger for this new feeling, which he could use when he wanted to act differently in the real world. The trigger would reinforce his Permissions.

6. Imagine Getting Approval and Support

Bill also mentally rehearsed getting approval for his new changes. As mentioned, he was going to remain closed mouthed with certain people who he knew would react with confusion or discomfort. But he had some friends who already were encouraging him to open up. He would go to them for strokes. He also rehearsed giving himself that great big hug he gave himself in step 4.

7. Practice in the Real World. Use Your Trigger

At his first opportunity, Bill practiced with his friends, giving genuine compliments and asking for needed help. He felt especially satisfied when he turned down a woman who asked for a loan. She already owed him a large sum of money.

Whenever he tensed up (after all he was breaking old injunctions), he fired his trigger and felt loose again.

The more Bill practiced, the easier it became, and he found his relationships much more rewarding. His friendships were deeper. He met a great woman and fell in love in a way that was a new experience for him. "I'm in love with my best friend," he confided to me. "Now life is really worth living."

With these powerful methods, using either the Direct Permission or Redecision Techniques, depending on which one works best for you, you can now get rid of negative messages and take conscious control of your life.

9

How To Harness the Positive Power Hidden in Your Negative Personality Traits

So far, you have learned of the vast reservoir of assets and positive experiences at your command with triggers. In addition to this consciously accessible reservoir, you have untapped resources of strengths and abilities just below your conscious mind, waiting to be released.

The source of this additional reservoir will surprise you. Believe it or not, all the parts of your personality that you do not appreciate now and give nasty names to, such as "cowardice," "immaturity," "aggressiveness," "weakness," "anxiety," and "jealousy," are valuable parts of your personality.

UNDERSTANDING YOUR PERSONALITY'S GOAL-DIRECTED UNITS

You are an organization of complex personality traits, drives, urges, impulses, skills, bodily functions, thinking patterns, sensations, emotions, attitudes, and habits.

These are organized into Goal-Directed Personality Units, which we simply will call "units." These units are goal directed because each one works toward achieving its ends. Most units do their job without prodding or even attention from you. Indeed, most units act automatically, like the automatic pilot on an airplane. You are unaware of all their activities or goals. Understanding how these units work will help you learn how to harness any power that may become misdirected.

We are made up of an exquisite balance of these organized units. One of your organized units, for instance, watches over you and shifts your attention between conscious and unconscious states when you are performing a repetitive or well-known act.

An example of this unit's function is walking to the store. You may be engrossed in thoughts about tomorrow, while you unconsciously walk the familiar path. But when you come to a street you must cross, your consciousness is alerted so you may take into account oncoming traffic. This unit will also alert you when a moving object enters your field of vision, but, generally speaking, you can be mentally anywhere else, while your "walking unit" will make the innumerable adjustments needed to walk over the terrain.

In speaking about personality units, there is nothing mysterious intended — no suggestion of little people running around inside us, operating us like a crew that runs a complex ocean liner. Yet we are a magnificent organization and it sometimes seems as if we are constructed to operate in this way.

Like all organizations, harmonious interaction between all functions is important. Your personality units work harmoniously most of the time, each fulfilling its job. Your modest unit sees to it that you are decently dressed, your tactful one is gracious to friends, your self-respecting one insists upon your being treated properly. These units are semiconscious and enable us to be social beings. There are other units taking care of totally automatic and unconscious duties, such as heart rate, body temperature, and release of hormones and digestive juices.

Still other units keep your body comfortable (usually without bothering the conscious mind with details) by attending to shifting your body weight from a tired leg to a more rested one, or turning your head and focusing your eyes so you can track a moving object.

Others intrude into your awareness to remind you that it is time to eat, urinate, or rest.

Further up the scale of consciousness is the part of you that performs a skill that demands your best, such as competing in a contest of tennis, chess, or even Pac-Man. Your full alertness is engaged by your unit that plays as well as possible.

When discussing complex ideas or negotiating a deal (buying a house, selling your car, persuading your spouse to move to another section of the country), a highly conscious part of your personality is active. You are well acquainted with these units.

Regardless of how your units are organized, conflicts are inevitable. For example, part of you may have wished to sleep later some Monday morning, but another part wanted to get a full paycheck. Life is full of these mundane conflicts. But sometimes we are faced with critical problems. Many soldiers struggle with the conflict between parts of them that want to defend their country and other parts that find the act of killing abhorrent and recoil at the idea of taking a human life.

A fascinating way to highlight conflicted personality units was developed by Fritz Perls, the late famous Gestalt therapist. He amazed psychologists when he introduced the "Double Chair Technique."

Perls' clients, sitting in one chair, would imagine a part of themselves in an empty chair, which was placed in front of them, and carry on a discussion with that part. This method of dramatizing personality units in action helped make them apparent, so clients could understand them better.

In such an exchange, a client would work on something he was having problems with, such as a jealous unit. The client would tell that part what he thought and felt about it. Then the client would change seats and answer as the jealous trait.

The client often would be so exasperated by a troublesome unit, such as an overly jealous one, that he would try to get rid of it.

CORRECTING ONE MAJOR MISTAKE CAN HELP YOU UNLOCK HIDDEN ASSETS

If you are like most people, you too have been battling and suppressing parts of your personality in the mistaken belief that they are defects in you. However, you have been blind to their value. Trying to get rid of personality units is a mistake. Correcting this one major mistake may be the most important thing you can do to unlock hidden strengths, gain new personal power, and stop wasting valuable energy.

In this and later chapters, you will learn how, by harnessing the power of formerly alienated units, clients achieved the following results:

A jealous lover used to go into rages and falsely accuse his fiancee of cheating on him. Each time he did this, he regretted his behavior. For years he tried to reform. Finally, on the verge of losing his fiancee forever, he learned in one day how to use this same energy to attract her to him more closely instead of driving her away.

A hard-driving executive was able to change his disabling migraine headaches into comfortable signals to warn him when it was time to take a much needed rest. A long-standing, self-defeating style of trying to push on in spite of the headaches—which only made them worse—was changed overnight into a system that allowed this man to accomplish twice as much by pacing himself correctly.

A businessman learned to handle business deals more successfully, without warring within himself. An attitude that caused a lifetime of inner turmoil was changed in twenty minutes.

A quality controller was able to turn his self-defeating anxiety into effective enthusiasm. The meetings he had abhorred for years suddenly became fun.

Anxiety can be turned into excitement and enthusiasm; obsequiousness into charm, graciousness, or tact; pain into a mild signal alerting you to care for yourself; jealousy into a constructive, caring attitude; anger into the ability to stand up for yourself, get your needs met, or defend your loved ones; and stubbornness can be turned into perseverance, stability, or reliability.

THE REAL SECRET TO FINDING INNER STRENGTH

The key is to remember that *every unit exists for your benefit and is trying to help you.*

You need to realize that all units are valuable, even those that are causing problems. As I mentioned before, these problems seem like liabilities, but are only assets in disguise, hidden from you because they are being used in the wrong place, at the wrong time, or you do not realize how they are helping you.

Yes, every single unit is trying to work for your benefit—no exceptions.

This statement is so contrary to the way most people view themselves that it is truly a secret.

HOW JACK UNDERMINED HIMSELF BY NOT UNDERSTANDING THIS SECRET

A man at one of my seminars, named Jack, reacted strongly when I presented this idea. "That's baloney," he blurted out. "There are parts of me that just get in my way. I'd be better off without them." He went on to say he has been battling most of his adult life trying to get rid of certain parts of his personality that were blocking him from being the kind of person he wanted to be. He described it as a "constant battle." He obviously had inner conflict. Sometimes he would "win" and other times he would "become weak and lose."

He explained, "I have to battle this 'weak guy' part who wants to be liked by everyone. Right now, I'm worried you won't like me because I am challenging your ideas. When I give in to this 'weak guy,' I never get my needs met. When negotiating a contract in my appliance business, I get a poor deal because I'm always afraid that asking for what I want might make the other guy dislike me. Sometimes I do just that; to be liked, I concede important points on a deal. On top of that, I'm so busy arguing inside myself when dealing with an important client that I get confused and make mistakes. I lost big money on some transactions. My business is suffering. I'd be a lot better off if I could just get rid of that part of my personality."

"I have to admire how well you have analyzed what's going on inside of you," I replied. "I'm sure this understanding has been of help to you, but you can benefit even more with a little further understanding.

"Right now," I continued, "I can't help thinking of the countless numbers of people who have made a fortune from getting others to like them. And I'm wondering how many good deals that 'weak guy' part of you has gotten for you without your realizing it."

I knew I had made a meaningful connection with him when Jack's face flushed. He looked as if a light had gone on in his mind. This man had consumed huge amounts of energy with his system of controlling his conflict. Although it worked for him (he was a successful businessman, husband, and father), he would be even further ahead by understanding the worth and value of that "weak guy" he fought against. Instead of fighting this personality trait that wanted to please people, Jack could make that unit his friend and ally.

To make this change, Jack had to learn how to communicate with this part that he called a "weak guy." In the next chapter, you will learn how Jack used the Inner Power Generator to do this and turn his "weak guy" unit into a valuable ally. This made Jack a better negotiator, a better friend, and gave him inner peace and satisfaction.

TRYING TO "GET RID OF" TROUBLESOME TRAITS IS A MISTAKE

Before using the Inner Power Generator, he needed to change his attitude and understand how trying to get rid of personality traits is a mistake and leads to poor results.

To help convince him of this, I told him the following true story. It is one of the stranger cases I have known.

Many years ago, when I was still a student, I met the most self-abasing man I ever saw. Physically, he was a mature, handsomely lean man with dark wavy hair touched with gray at the temples. If I were to have cast him for a film strictly because of his looks, I would have made him a high-level diplomat or an advisor to a king. But his demeanor was woeful. He hung his head, and his eyes had a pained expression. He was, however, hyperalert and scrutinized my face for any signs of rejection. He complained how no one, not even his wife and daughters, listened to him or considered his needs. He did acknowledge that this might be because, instead of telling them what he wanted, he always agreed to everything they wanted. This was his frantic effort to avoid disapproval.

I didn't see this man again until three years later. I was sitting in my office when I heard someone in the waiting room loudly insisting that he wanted to see me. No, he didn't have an appointment, he told the secretary, and he marched right into my office. I was astounded to see the man I knew as a student. He was now loud, demanding, and abrasive. I learned that his wife had left him and that his children would have nothing to do with him. His reason for coming to see me? To show me how well he was doing!

In three years, he had acquired an armor of steely self-confidence that insulated him from considering the feelings of others.

Both units — the accommodating one that was sensitive to the needs of others and the aggressive one that looked out for his self-serving needs — were valuable. However, one without the other created a caricature of a human being.

Somehow, instead of developing the needed unit and blending it with the one he already had, this man eliminated one for the other. This happened because somehow he got the mistaken idea that one of these units was "bad,"and he had enough will power to subdue it—even though it usually is impossible to subdue a part of your personality so completely.

HOW CHARLES HARNESSED THE POWER OF HIS ANXIETY TO BECOME A PERSUASIVE LEADER

In contrast, a happy result was achieved when a quality controller named Charles learned to accept and cooperate with a part of himself that he hated and considered a negative trait.

When I first met Charles, he hated the anxiety he felt before and during a business meeting. Such meetings were needed often. He was responsible for quality control in the manufacture of large appliances and he was good at his job. One of his duties was to convince his business colleagues, who were also involved in manufacturing the appliances, to adopt the procedures needed to ensure that their stoves and refrigerators were well made.

At his request, I hypnotized him so that he felt calm and peaceful at those meetings. But it worked too well. At the next meeting, he was calm — and dull. Charles didn't persuade a single person present of the worth of his ideas. He had always been alert and lively at these meetings.

It was then that he realized the true value of his anxiety. It could be used as excitement and enthusiasm to make him persuasive and effective at those meetings. As any modern salesman knows, enthusiasm sells.

Charles was a changed man. He now welcomed his feelings at those meetings and harnessed the power of his anxiety to motivate his colleagues. He tingled with excitement. It was infectious and the other workers looked to him for leadership. Instead of dreading the meetings, Charles became eager to attend so he could exercise his new-found power.

However, most people, when they try to "improve" themselves, struggle to get rid of their "faults." For instance, one man, who thought he was too proud, tried to rid himself of this trait. He was alert to stamp out all expressions and feelings of pride. He would catch himself in the act, like a truant officer catching a delinquent playing hooky from school. Seeing each expression of pride as a failure, he would psychologically nag himself into a depression. Then he would set his jaw in firm resolve to do better. Finally, after years of tenacious effort, he reached his goal and had stamped out every speck of that particular "deadly sin." At this point, just when he was reveling in his success, he suddenly realized he is now proud of not being proud. Having lost his humility, he was undone—a fallen angel.

The above account is typical. If you are like most people, you try to "improve" yourself by trying to suppress or get rid of certain units. This is especially true if you try to be perfect. You may try not to be impatient, lazy, or shy. But, with this system of self-improvement, the internal nagging is constant. If these private thoughts could be wired to loudspeakers, this self-criticism would make an ear-splitting din.

What a tiring and exhausting way to live! Not that self-criticism doesn't work. Like all parts, it can be extremely valuable. But the constant effort to eliminate a quality consumes too much energy. Truly successful men and women don't do it this way. They use criticism like garlic, just a little bit so you hardly know it's there. And, just as the right amount of garlic improves the flavor of food, the right amount of criticism improves our final product.

Those who value all parts of their personality use criticism sparingly. Most successful people consistently respect, appreciate, and use all of their parts.

However, they do this unconsciously. When researchers asked how they achieve their success, successful people gave various descriptions of how they think they succeed. They described only the small piece of success strategy that is available to their consciousness.

And sometimes what they thought was that the relevant strategy was not really it. "Develop sound judgment to do the right thing at the right time." That is the "secret"of a past president of the Metropolitan Life Insurance Company. It sounds impressive and as if he's saying something specific, but it's like saying "Always do the right thing," or "Don't make mistakes." Such obvious advice is not helpful. It is a rationalization.

But a true, basic reason for their success lay hidden from them. The researchers found the basic reason was that instead of working at cross purposes, their units work together. They have the power that comes from inner harmony. Although they achieved their happy state more by good fortune than conscious effort, you now have an advantage. You can understand these principles and use them to promote your own success.

However, personality conflicts usually cannot be smoothed out simply by looking at them as assets, but it is a necessary beginning. You need to go further and understand specifically what these troublesome units are trying to help you accomplish, and how you can rechannel their efforts.

The quality control man was able to understand his unit's purpose—giving him energy to be persuasive—fairly easily. But often the unit's goal is harder to learn.

The next chapter will show you specifically how to gain this understanding, redirect your misguided units to work cooperatively within your personality structure, and achieve the power of inner harmony.

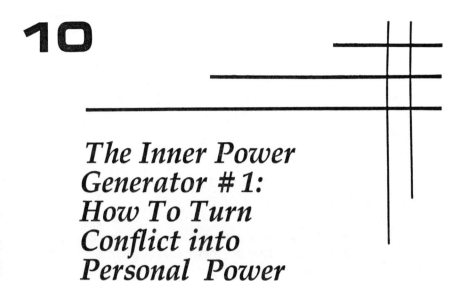

The Inner Power Generator #1: How To Turn Conflict into Personal Power

Decreasing inner conflict by getting your units to work together harmoniously will benefit you immensely. It will increase your energy. You will feel like doing countless new things with your life. Your efficiency and effectiveness will be improved so you will perform much better. As you have seen in the previous chapter, you can turn a liability into an asset, a negative into a plus — like Charles, the quality control expert, turned his anxiety into enthusiasm, or the lover turned his jealous behavior into charming behavior, or the headache sufferer turned his pain into a signal which guarded his health.

THE POWER OF YOUR GOAL-DIRECTED PERSONALITY UNITS

As a member of a species designed to survive, you are born with all of the resources you need. The key is to be able to tap these resources when you need them and keep your units working together as a team. As you recall, the achievement of such harmony rests upon the principle that all of your units are there to help you.

Even conflict is no exception to the rule. It is the valuable weighing and assessing of alternatives. For example, Jack's conflict between being hard nosed or being friendly was an attempt to solve a problem, even though his conflict also caused him turmoil and consumed valuable energy.

INNER HARMONY REDUCES SELF-DOUBT AND INCREASES SELF-CONFIDENCE

Besides freeing enormous amounts of energy, reducing inner conflict also reduces self-doubt and increases self-confidence. Without inner conflict, you don't give off the signals that can be seen in a person who is conflicted. As a part of him objects to what he is doing, he shows discord in his behavior. Warring units show up as inconsistent behavior. One piece of behavior does not match another.

You are already familiar with this. Looking for such discrepancies is the basic tactic you use to test out if someone is lying. You watch for evasive eyes or listen for hesitant speech or some other sign that a part of him is not in accord with what he is saying.

With your conflicts minimized, not only will you enjoy the feelings generated by self-confidence, all your actions will be consistent with what you are saying. Therefore, other people will immediately sense your assurance. They will be more inclined to listen to your ideas and consider your suggestions. You will be more persuasive. With this increase in your ability to get your ideas accepted, your personal power with people will increase.

Not only will you enjoy the sense of inner peace created by having your units in harmony, it is well researched that your physical health will also benefit, since you will be less prone to stress related diseases.

Finally, once you've gained a high enough level of harmony, you will start achieving higher levels of intuition and creativity.

THE THREE GOLDEN RULES FOR GAINING INNER POWER

To reap the benefits of inner power and marshal your natural assets so you can reshape your life, you need to follow the three principles I have been explaining:

1. Every part is trying to help you.
2. Accept the good intention of every part and help it fill its good intention.
3. Every behavior you have can be made useful and rechanneled into positive activity.

At one of my classes, a woman objected. She could see no positive value in suicidal behavior. "Killing yourself is simply wrong," she said. "Your loved ones, who are left behind, are devastated. There is no way to reverse your suicide. You are dead."

"Yes, the results you describe are bad, but the intent is much different. Usually, someone commits suicide to end pain—either physical or mental. At the time, they cannot see any other way to do this. Certainly, ending pain is a desirable goal. The task is to find another way to stop hurting. The Triple Split Technique, and others that have been given earlier, are designed to help do this.

"Sometimes," I went on, "people make suicidal gestures to draw attention to their plight and get help. I know several people who have done this to get their spouses to realize the seriousness of their marital problem.

"One woman had a husband who was a workaholic," I continued. "He neglected her terribly. Her inability to convince him to give her more of himself drove her to act rashly. She overdosed. However, she had misjudged and almost died. Her husband was shocked and finally realized how important it was for him to spend time with her and give her some loving care.

"It's a shame," I commented, "that someone has to go to the extreme of showing that they are willing to kill themselves before their plight is taken seriously. In this woman's case, it worked. She convinced him."

"What about murder, what can be positive about that?" someone else asked.

"As much as I abhor murder even more than suicide, murder also has a positive intent," I answered. "A jealous husband murders his wife's lover because he wants his wife to himself—or an heiress, who murders to get her inheritance earlier, wants money. Not necessarily bad things to want. When you separate the behavior from the intent, you find that the behavior is negative but the intent is positive.

Although murder and suicide are extreme examples. Most of us have more benign concerns that are important to us.

Whenever you have trouble stopping some action or habit of yours, it's a safe bet that action or habit is trying to do something for you and is needed. To just take the unit away would cripple your personality. You simply need to replace the unwanted behavior with a better way to meet that unit's need.

To begin with, you need to talk to yourself to find out about the unit's intention. That's right, I said talk to yourself.

But how do you talk to an intangible 'unit'? Simply go inside yourself, as you do when thinking to yourself, having an internal dialogue, or daydreaming. Identify the unit in charge of creating the behavior in question and thank that system for what it is trying to achieve, even if you wish it had a better way of achieving its goal.

This suggestion may seem a little strange, like talking to the supernatural. However, there is really nothing strange or mysterious about it. You talk to yourself all the time. It is a useful skill for making plans or evaluating something.

When deciding whether to go to a show, for instance, you might say to yourself something like, "That picture got good reviews and I want to see it." But you may also feel tired that night and answer yourself back, "I'm too tired tonight. I'll see it another time." These are two of your units having a dialogue. One part wants to be entertained and the other wants you to rest.

Another common example is the athlete criticizing himself for a mistaken play. You probably have seen a tennis player scowl and look at his hand after just missing a shot. You might even see his lips move. His "coaching" unit is talking to his "playing" unit.

Sometimes you use pictures and feeling more than words when you think to yourself, so the right term would be *communicate* instead of *talk*.

For instance, when deciding on which car to buy, you will not only carry on an internal dialogue with yourself, but also imagine pictures of the car: how it will look in your driveway and the reactions of others who see you in it. You will imagine the feeling of driving it down the highway. Also, you may compare the feeling you have, if you decide not to buy it, with the feeling you have if you do decide to buy it.

Clearly then, communicating with your units in the way I am suggesting is little different from the common ways we communicate with ourselves when we are doing other kinds of thinking. You are simply not used to talking to yourself in the way I am now instructing you do.

THE SECRET WISDOM OF YOUR PERSONALITY UNITS

Unconscious parts usually are right on target. I know several driven workaholics who push themselves until a headache forces them to take a much needed rest. Headaches can serve various needs. One woman's "sick headaches" drove her into seclusion, serving to stop her from having painful arguments with her husband. Her headaches were less painful to her than arguing with him. A handsome minister got a headache whenever a pretty parishioner became sexually seductive and too tempting for him. Not only headaches, but most behaviors we call symptoms are trying to serve some useful purpose. Parts keep their intention out of your awareness for a good reason: You might try to stop their important work.

After spending a few weeks making peace overtures to your personality units, you probably will have resolved your simpler conflicts and noticed improvement in some areas of your life already. It's surprising how much energy you save when you stop warring with yourself. To resolve those systems still in discord, you will need a more sophisticated technique, called The Inner Power Generator, to bring the conflicting parts into harmony with the rest of your personality. But first you need to find out what type of conflict you are having.

WHAT TYPE OF CONFLICT DO YOU HAVE?

When you have inner conflict, which is a more common way of saying that a unit's goals are being interfered with, you will be uncomfortable. You will have some or all of the following signs: trouble falling asleep, trouble concentrating, trouble making decisions, or trouble listening to someone else because you're having an imaginary conversation going on inside your head. Physical symptoms such as teeth grinding, muscular tension, headache, or queasy stomach are other signs of conflict. Usually, you simply feel nervous and uptight.

For instance, a chef in a large hotel was being treated disrespectfully by his new boss. The chef suppressed his outraged because he believed showing anger was beneath his dignity. However, this frustrated the part of his personality that wanted to use anger to protect his self-esteem. He lost a lot of sleep over this. Also, he held imaginary conversations inside his head in which the boss at last recognized the chef's value and apologized. However, this compulsive daydreaming interfered with his concentration at work and he did not do as well.

Another woman felt nauseous because she believed it would be disrespectful for her to go against her mother's wishes. Her mother wanted her to marry a man she did not love.

These are outward signs of conflict of which there are two main types. The simpler type are conflicts in which two parts are competing with each other. What each of them do is clearly good for you, but they get in each other's way. Each part is doing something helpful, but they do it at the same time, or at the wrong time.

Jack's case is an example of the first type. The friendly, generous unit he had called "weak guy" was overactive during business deals. What he did not realize was this very same unit made him popular with his friends. Furthermore, his wife confided in him that this was one of the traits that attracted him to her. Unfortunately, sometimes Jack's other system, which looked after his interests and tried to drive a good deal, also would become active at the wrong times.

For instance, he found himself becoming competitive with his own son, who was only eleven years old. Jack rationalized that he was "only trying to toughen him up and prepare him for the real world." However, in his heart, Jack knew he was not being a good father at those times.

One of Jack's units looked out for Jack and saw to it he took care of his interests, while the other helped him be a good friend, father, and husband. These are both valuable things and most people have workable ways of achieving these goals. In Jack's case, however, when both units tried to be in charge and do their job at the wrong time, they got in each other's way and neither could do their job well.

The second type of conflict occurs when a part stops you from doing something that is good, or makes you do something that seems harmful.

Examples of the second type are: jealous rages, headaches, overeating, excessive worry, smoking, anxiety, excessive anger.

These reactions are harmful but usually are the lesser of two evils. As we saw, the jealous lover would have been indifferent to his fiancee and would have lost her that way. Without their headaches, the wife would have had marital arguments, the minister may have been seduced, and the hard-driving executive would have driven himself to nervous exhaustion. Overeating has helped some people ward off depression. I know of three cases where being fat kept people from having illicit sexual affairs.

One of the most useful and powerful techniques known is called the *Inner Power Generator #1.* It can resolve inner conflict and release tremendous power that otherwise would have been misdirecterd and wasted. There are two versions of this technique: Inner Power Generator #1 and Inner Power Generator #2. Version 1 is for resolving the first type of conflict—useful activity occurring at the wrong times. Version 2 is for conflicts of the second type—activity which has no apparent useful purpose.

Jack's type of conflict meets the criteria for Inner Power Generator #1. Separately, getting his needs met and being a friend are both good. However, when he's watching out for his needs in a contract negotiation, he feels discord.

HOW JACK USED THE INNER POWER GENERATOR TO TURN A "WEAKNESS" INTO A STRENGTH

In addition to the discussion with Jack described in the last chapter, I did some further work with him that will serve to illustrate how to use the Inner Power Generator #1. You will recall Jack thought he had a "weak guy" unit that was interfering with his business deals. Jack wanted to stop having this interference.

I asked Jack to imagine himself negotiating a contract with a business associate and experiencing his conflict. I suggested that he press down on his left leg when he had a good three-channel image. When he did this, I asked him to get in touch with the part of his personality that wanted to be conciliatory, and ask this unit what it was trying to do for him.

Jack closed his eyes to shut out distractions and asked aloud, "Hey, weak guy, what are you trying to do to me?"

"No, no," I interrupted him, "don't call it names. Just ask it if it is willing to communicate with us. The first step is to set up a communication channel with it."

Jack followed my instructions, but reported he got a, "No," in his verbal channel.

"It's no wonder. After all, you two have been battling for years. If you want the unit's help, you have to gain its trust. Go inside and tell it you don't want to get rid of it. You want to help the unit do its job."

Jack agreed, did as I suggested, and reported the unit told him that it didn't want Jack to turn into a Scrooge who drove away all his friends with his greed. Jack was stunned. "I know better than that. But I guess I need that unit to make sure I don't go that far."

"Tell it that," I said, "and negotiate a deal with it that you will consider its concerns and be careful. You can start by giving it a nicer nickname and being its friend."

Jack went ahead, and reported that he now appreciates the part he calls "Buddy." They made a deal that he would pay attention to Buddy. Whenever negotiating a contract, Jack would decide whether Buddy's suggestions to concede points on the contract were good ideas or not, and act accordingly. He negotiated another deal with his personality systems. Buddy was to be in charge in social situations. The part that looked after Jack's interests was to serve only in an advisory capacity.

"How does that feel?" I asked.

"It feels good," he replied with enthusiasm.

"Fine. Now, make a trigger for your new program by pressing down on your right leg. Whenever you feel that conflict, fire your trigger to change back to this harmonious state."

As in all the reprogramming methods, Jack ended with mentally rehearsing the new program. Using the plan he worked out with Buddy, Jack imagined in all his channels making deals with various businessmen while paying attention to Buddy as a valued advisor. Then Jack imagined himself attending social gatherings and having Buddy in charge.

This change had a dramatic effect on Jack's life. He still went after a good deal on contracts, but he tempered his outlook with humanity. He enjoyed improved relationships with his business associates and his company prospered. His home life also benefitted. Jack built a better relationship with his son. By using this new system he gained a new sense of power and control over his life.

Conflict over spending versus saving is another example of competing parts doing helpful things, but at the wrong time. One unit wants to enjoy the fruits of your labor now, when another wants to save it for something special, like a dream vacation or unexpected emergencies.

Think of the times you had a tug-of-war with yourself when you were deciding whether or not to buy something. You stand in front of that television with its thirty-six-inch-chromex-truer-than-life-color picture tube and quadraphonically-enhanced-high-fidelity-stereo-phonic-sound poly-speakers. You want it. Or you're looking at that tastefully understated suit, or that glittering, jewelled gold watch, or that two-inch-thick prime-cut steak and, before you can tell the clerk "gimme," a small voice creeps into your head and whispers, "Do you really need it? Can't you get something less expensive? Think of all the money you can save if you don't buy it."

Other common examples of units doing perfectly acceptable actions, but stepping on each other's toes, include wanting to be playing when you are working and, the opposite situation, feeling guilty when you are playing.

Salesmen who work outside the office on commission are especially prone to this conflict. What can be a wonderful freedom—choosing your own working hours and being able to take a day off when you want—becomes an uncomfortable burden for some people. Students who choose their study hours are in a similar situation. Of course, some workers can feel this conflict even if their hours are regulated by their workplace. They sit in their office, wishing they could play. Then, on the weekend, they spoil their fun by worrying about all the work they didn't get done. These people need to have these conflicting units work at different times and keep out of each other's way so they can work when they work and play when they play.

There are insomniacs who lie awake making great plans for the next day; but, when tomorrow comes, they are too tired to carry them out. Negotiating when to plan and when to sleep works in these cases.

In addition to conflicts caused by parts competing between giving or taking, saving or spending, and working or playing, there are conflicts between sleeping or planning, speaking or listening, among others. These types of conflict lend themselves to resolution by the short Inner Power Generator #1.

HOW TO USE THE INNER POWER GENERATOR #1: STEP BY STEP

Step 1: Choose Your Target

To use the Inner Power Generator #1 yourself, start by selecting a conflict to work on. Choose one which has two useful but competing parts.

Step 2: Establish Communication

Since we know the "problem" is doing something important for you, or at the very least trying to, you will need to find out what the unit's true purpose is. Although it may seem self-evident, do not take for granted that you understand the unit's purpose. It might surprise you. One hard-driving architect thought his part which strove to do everything perfectly was trying to make him do high-quality work. Instead, when he used the Power Generator and asked his perfectionistic part what it was trying to do for him, he learned that its real purpose was different. It was trying to get love in the form of approval for his work. Not just ordinary approval, but approval unmarred by any criticism.

A straightforward way of finding the true purpose is to go right to the "boss," the unit that's creating the behavior you consider a problem. The boss doesn't think this behavior is a problem. The boss thinks it is a solution.

To get to the boss, imagine yourself experiencing your conflict. When you do this, be in the imagined situation—don't be an observer watching yourself. Make a good three-channel image and make a trigger, such as pressing down on your left leg. As you hold that trigger, go inside yourself and get in touch with the boss, the unit that wants to continue doing things the old way.

Use the general word *communicate* instead of "tell" or "show." For instance, you might ask the part to talk to you or show pictures to you. However, you do not know what channel the unit uses. It might want to express itself to you, but in some other channel. Units specialize in channels more than people do, so you're more apt to get an answer if you let the unit choose its channel of communication. You can stay in your verbal channel.

(Also, you might ask that unit what it does for you without first asking if it will to talk to you. You may not get an answer, however. If that unit trusted you with its business, it probably would have let you know long before now.)

When you ask it to communicate with you, be alert for some response. The answer can be in any of the five channels. Usually, it is a straightforward word or picture.

Step 3: Establish Trust

If it refuses to answer, reassure that unit you are not trying to get rid of it, but want to help it do its job better.

Step 4: Find Out Its Purpose

When it agrees, ask it what its intent is. What is it trying to do for you?

When you find out your unit's true purpose, do the same thing with the other interfering unit. Establish communication and trust, and ask the competing system what it is trying to do for you.

Step 5: Negotiate between Parts

You often can work out a good compromise. You would be surprised how many personality units simply want to be acknowledged and have their opinion considered. It's as if the more you try to ignore them, the louder they become, like little children. Of course, units may not use the hearing channel; so, instead of getting louder, they may increase your fear or tire you out, trying to get you to pay attention to them.

Like Jack did with his business unit and "nice guy" unit, negotiate when each one can be active. Ask each when it thinks it is most needed. Jack's business unit thought its job was most important when making business deals, while "nice guy" thought social events were its main responsibility.

Ask each of your competing units if they would like to do their job without interference from the other. When they agree that they would not like to be bothered, ask each one if it is willing not to bother the other in return for the same consideration. In other words, get them to agree each would give the other the same treatment and each would respect the other's area of responsibility.

Ask them to agree to cooperate this way in the future. If either one becomes dissatisfied with the new arrangement, the dissatisfaction would be a signal that a new arrangement needs to be made. This would be done by renegotiation. Nothing lasts forever. As a circuit judge once said when granting a "permanent" injunction, "This injunction is as permanent as a permanent wave."

Finally, make a trigger for whatever deal you agree on, and mentally rehearse the new program. Use the principles you have learned: Use three or more channels and imagine yourself inside the picture, not watching yourself do it.

TAPPING THE WISDOM OF YOUR UNCONSIOUS

I have been using the idea of an unconscious and conscious mind throughout this book. Your conscious mind has the feeling of being you. When I use the term *you,* I am addressing your conscious mind. The idea of an unconscious mind is similar to my concept of units. Although your conscious mind is an organized system that tries to be consistent, I don't think there is one unified unconscious mind, just different systems within us taking care of us without our being very aware of them. Furthermore, your conscious mind is much less automatic and has to think things through before acting, like learning to drive. As you develop, through repetition, automatic ways of doing things, like learning to drive well, they become semi-unconscious parts of your personality and relieve you from having to concentrate while performing such tasks.

Other systematic activities are more deeply buried and not easily reached by your conscious mind, probably because these units were developed when you were so young or, possibly, you were born with them. Some of these units do extremely useful things, like saving your feelings from being hurt, or maintaining your sense of self-worth.

The important thing about units is that they have information and abilities that your everyday state of consciousness does not. If you stop and think about it, you have units that are stronger than your conscious "you." To show yourself the power of your unconscious, try to use a new name for a day. You can tell your friends what you are doing, so they will not get confused and they can help you with this experiment. Try to introduce yourself only by your new name. Also, try to not respond to someone calling you by your real name. Sooner or later, someone will call you by your real name and you will unconsciously react. Even if you suppress any outward signs, you will feel yourself respond internally.

If your units were not stronger than your everyday way of thinking, you would have effortlessly made all the changes in yourself that your conscious mind wants.

The point of this is twofold: Your various units have knowledge and wisdom beyond your conscious mind and often these systems are more capable than your conscious mind of reaching certain goals. If you try to follow the reprogramming systems such as the Power Generator with only your ordinary consciousness (trying to figure out the part's purpose and alternate ways of satisfying its purpose instead of involving your relevant units and getting their answers) it will not work. You will be missing important information. Secondly, your units are powerful and will undermine and defeat any attempts at change which conflict with their goals. Conversely, with your unit's cooperation, you have an experienced and skilled ally helping you make the change.

OUTLINE FOR POWER GENERATOR #1

1. Imagine your conflict. Make a trigger for it and get in touch with the responsible part.
2. Ask it to communicate with you.
3. Establish trust. If necessary, reassure it of your respect and good will.
4. Ask what it's trying to do for you.
5. Negotiate a way to reach common goals. Make a trigger for the new agreement.
6. Mentally rehearse your new program.

Follow this outline of the version of Inner Power General #1 to change competing parts to cooperating parts. Select one conflict to change at a time. In essence, you negotiate between the parts and make whatever trades are needed. Install the new program and practice it in the real world until your improved system becomes a habit. Then you may start work on changing another conflict. You might have two or three. Remember to start with the easiest one and work up to the hardest.

11

The Inner Power Generator #2: Replace Bad Habits with Positive Actions

Have you ever had the discouraging experience of trying to stop a bad habit, but failing repeatedly? Maybe, you often lose your temper only to find yourself losing valuable friends and damaging your family life as well. Or maybe you've tried to go on a diet, but after some success at the start, you rebound right back to your old eating habits *and* your old weight. In spite of sincere resolves to stop, *you keep on doing it* — whether "it" is flying off the handle or opening the refrigerator door too often, the problem is the same. If you find yourself perpetuating bad habits, you are experiencing a particular type of conflict. Yet, luckily, this type of conflict responds well to a technique I call the Inner Power Generator #2.

Besides conflicts caused by helpful behavior happening at the wrong time (as discussed in the previous chapter), there are conflicts of this second type: A personality unit is pursuing its hidden goal in a way that is creating problems — such as overweight, hangovers, loss of friends, or lovers' quarrels. Although trying to be helpful to you, you can see *no* good coming from this behavior. The unit's way of trying to help you seems to cause only discomfort or pain and often harms others as well.

Freud called the hidden, beneficial results his patients derived

151

from their symptoms "secondary gain," and he understood the power of personality units that worked toward achieving such gains. Simply removing unwanted behavior (which he did at one time by giving his hypnotized patients direct suggestions to stop) rarely works. The symptom usually reappears, or a worse one takes its place. This is called "symptom substitution." This happens because, when you stop a part from gaining its goals, it will find another, possibly more harmful, way to achieve them. You have, most likely, had the experience of watching a friend stop a bad habit, such as smoking or drinking, and find that he becomes irritable, has trouble sleeping, or becomes depressed.

HOW THE INNER POWER GENERATOR #2 HELPS YOU REPLACE BAD HABITS WITH CONSTRUCTIVE ACTION

The new techniques presented in this book take the important fact of symptom substitution into account by respecting all the parts of your personality and their aims. Instead of simply stopping an unwanted behavior, the Inner Power Generator #2 substitutes a desirable behavior.

Instead of trying to deprive your personality by frustrating a unit which is trying to help you, the Power Generator Programmer #2 adds another facet to your personality: the ability to fulfill your needs in ways that are both effective and harmonious with all your personality systems.

This produces profound personality changes that are long lasting and stable because the technique respects your inner dynamics — the exquisite balance of personality units pursuing their individual goals.

The Power Generator #2 includes a technique for finding new ways of filling your hidden needs. These new ways have to meet two standards: They have to be at least as effective as the old ways (the symptom), and they have to be acceptable to all aspects of your personality. By enabling you to change your behaviors in ways that continue to meet the needs of all of your units (or at least not interfere with the workings of other systems), it increases the likelihood for success enormously and eliminates symptom substitution.

Carl: The Jealous Lover

To illustrate how this is done, let me tell you how Carl, whose jealous rages were driving away his fiancee, became charming and attracted her to him instead.

Carl was a brilliant engineer who emigrated to the United States and left his wife in Germany until he was settled. Unfortunately, she suddenly became ill and died before he could send for her.

After a suitable period of mourning, Carl began a relationship with a wonderful woman named Lisa, but he began to have a problem that threatened to destroy his new-found happiness. He was becoming terribly jealous of Lisa. He tortured himself with doubts and verbally flayed his fiancee with accusations for hours at a time.

Carl and his German wife had grown up in a small traditional German village where the roles of men and women were clearly separated. Carl's wife had been "an old-fashioned girl" and, as such, had socialized mostly with women. Like most of the women in her village, she related to men, other than her husband, in a polite and carefully limited way.

Carl's problem emerged when he began dating American women who, appropriate to their culture, were friendly with men. He would feel jealous and moderately uncomfortable, but was able to tolerate it. But when he fell in love with Lisa, who was bright and outgoing, Carl just couldn't get used to her being warm and friendly to other men. The discomfort he had felt with his other dates grew to hideous proportions when it came to the woman he loved. He became obsessed with his jealousy.

Lisa was true to Carl, and he was in no danger of losing her — at least not to another man. But, ironically, his doubts and bitter accusations were threatening to drive her away. Carl was no fool. His conscious mind knew the damage he was doing. He also knew that his fiancee's behavior was perfectly acceptable in America, but he couldn't put an end to his jealous rages. At our session, Carl told me that he wanted to stop his jealous behavior. This was his target.

Since Carl was in obvious conflict and wanted to replace destructive behavior with desirable behavior, he used Inner Power Generator #2 to reach his goal.

HOW CARL USED THE INNER POWER GENERATOR #2
TO TRANSFORM HIS JEALOUS BEHAVIOR INTO CHARM

At our session, I told Carl, "Go inside yourself and recall a time you felt extremely jealous and get in touch with the unit that makes you feel that way."

Carl closed his eyes and nodded that he had contacted his jealous feelings.

"Now, ask that part if it is willing to communicate with you," I instructed. Notice, I advised him to ask only for communication, nothing more. This way, he would be asking for a simple "yes" or "no" answer, and would be more apt to get a response to this kind of simple request. It is essential that communication is opened up so you can proceed.

Carl shook his head and said, "I hear a 'no,'" indicating that this unit used the verbal channel. However, it objected to talking to Carl because it did not trust him.

"Reassure that unit you are not trying to get rid of it, but respect it and want to help it do its job better," I said.

Carl gave me a look that seemed to be asking if I were insane. After all, he had been having a terrible time with that unit of his personality. It had been torturing him endlessly. But he trusted me and said aloud to that unit, "I don't want to get rid of you. I want to do things better. Now will you talk to me?"

His head nodded unconsciously and then he said, "Yes, it will." Usually, an onlooker will see signals that give the answer before the person himself is aware of it. This is of interest to clinicians and you need not be concerned when you program yourself.

"O.K. Just for kicks, let's nickname it J.P. for jealous personality," I kidded. "Now ask J.P. what it is trying to do for you."

"What are you trying to do for me?" Carl asked. After a pause, Carl reported what he had heard: "It is trying to get me to do my best to keep from losing Lisa." Then, he added, "And I thought it was just trying to make me miserable." Carl now understood, and even though he disliked how the unit was going about it, he agreed with what it was trying to do.

"Ask J.P.," I continued to coach Carl, "whether, if it knew of a better way of doing its job—helping you to keep Lisa—would it be willing to use that better way?" The offer of something better is irresistible. It is essential to get this unit involved and agreeable to change.

Carl reported a "yes" answer.

Notice how we are respecting this unit and checking whether it agrees to each step before we go ahead. Riding roughshod over your unconscious is foolish and won't work.

Next, in keeping with the principle to respect all units, I had Carl thank "J.P." Then I hold him to contact his creative units and ask them if they would be willing to help. All of us have creative abilities. You don't have to be creative in the artistic sense. You have been creatively molding your personality since you were born, and learned things like when to cry or laugh to get different responses from people.

After questioning his creative units as I had instructed, Carl reported, "I didn't get an answer. All that happened is I saw bright flashes of colored lights and shimmering forms all dancing around."

Carl had misunderstood. His creative systems were communicating with him in the visual channel. For whatever reason, they chose that channel instead of the verbal one Carl expected. Be alert for any response, not just a verbal one. It can be in any channel. If the response doesn't make immediate sense, you can usually make it understandable as a "yes-no" answer.

"Ask the creative units to make the lights bright for a 'yes' and dark for a 'no,'" I instructed.

"The lights are brighter," Carl said, after a while.

"Ask them if they are willing to show you other ways to help J.P. do its job," I instructed.

"Will you show me . . ."

"No," I interrupted Carl, "just ask if it is willing."

"Are you willing to show me other ways to help J.P. do its job?" Carl asked. When he reported he saw the bright lights, which meant "yes," I had him ask, "Will you show me *three* new ways to help J.P. do its job?"

Carl meditated for a while and I noticed his head nod three times. Then he reported that he was shown three new things he could do: marry Lisa, attract her to him by being as charming as he was when they first met, or threaten other men to stay away.

"Now go inside again and check with all your units and find out if any of them object to any of these new ways," I coached. This technique ensures harmony and helps you select behaviors that fit your unique personality. Solutions that would cause further conflict are eliminated here before they are acted on.

Carl closed his eyes and soon reported, "I'm not ready to marry yet and if I go around threatening men who like her—well that's no good. I don't want to do that."

"O.K., you have one conflict-free alternative. Check with J.P. and ask if it would be willing, whenever it gives you that jealous feeling, instead of attacking Lisa, to charm her and attract her to you."

Carl did so and got a "yes."

"Good. Now ask J.P. what it can use as a trigger, a signal to remind it to use its new choice," I instructed.

After consulting with his part, Carl reported it would use the first twinges of jealousy as a trigger for the new responses. "Now, whenever I feel those twinges of jealousy, they will be a trigger to remind me I have a new choice: to charm Lisa."

"Now, thank J.P. for being your friend and watching over you, so you won't lose the most precious thing in your world—Lisa," I said.

Carl followed these instructions and when he opened his eyes, he looked excited.

"How does that feel, Carl?"

"That feels wonderful," he exclaimed.

"Now close your eyes and rehearse your new program. Imagine yourself from now on seeing Lisa being friendly to men, feeling just a slight sensation of jealousy, remembering your new choice, and acting on it by charming Lisa."

Carl closed his eyes and rehearsed the following imaginary scenario. He saw, heard, and felt himself at parties and other social gatherings, and when he saw Lisa talking with a man, he felt a little jealous. Instead of sulking and saving his resentment to unleash at Lisa later, he thanked J.P. and joined Lisa and her friend and enjoyed competing for Lisa's attention. He imagined he and Lisa having many such delightful evenings.

Imagining that scene this way set up automatic triggers that would help him in the future. He reported that he knew Lisa would react well and he liked that.

Carl's new understanding that his jealous unit was urging him to do something to keep Lisa changed his self-image to a more positive one. Instead of hating that part, he liked and appreciated more of himself. He felt a new sense of mastery and confidence over his feelings about Lisa.

The session ended with Carl again thanking J.P. for his interest.

When I had a chance to ask Carl about his jealousy some months later, he acted a a little surprised and claimed he never really had a problem with jealousy. He said it was just the opposite. Just the other evening, he said, he was alone sitting on his sofa and began thinking about an incident that had happened at a restaurant some time earlier. He remembered Lisa laughing and having a good time with a man at their table. Carl got up from his sofa, went over to the phone, and called her. He delighted her with romantic talk and reassurances of love. "Now is that the way a jealous man would act?" he asked.

I hid my amusement at Carl's lapse of memory. Before working with the Power Generator, Carl would have remained worried and upset with his jealousy and been in a foul mood when Lisa and he met. His new program was so automatic and worked so well, he had forgotten the painful way he used to act.

His type of denial after using this personal power technique is not uncommon. I think, when this happens, it is because the unit is protecting the new system. Keeping it out of awareness prevents tampering by your conscious mind, which might interfere with the way it works now.

Lisa remembered how temperamental Carl had been and appreciated the change he had made. But, wisely, she went along with his denial and did not remind him of how jealous he used to be. Intuitively, she feared this might cause him to revert to his old system.

I suspect, but have no hard evidence, that another reason for Carl's denial had to do with his reluctance to think it might be possible for someone else to influence him so profoundly. People like to feel in control of themselves and they fear someone might, Svengali-like, control them. By denying that anything of great significance happened, Carl reduced the threat that I might be in "control" of him.

He felt that way although, when he went through the Power Programming system, he was really in control himself. I was only guiding him. Even though some people feel like I "did it" to them, I no more "reprogram" anybody than a television chef cooks your dinner when you follow his recipes in your kitchen.

And just as you can follow a recipe from a cookbook without the chef being there to help you, you can use the Inner Power Generator #2 yourself to reprogram your bad habits into constructive substitute activities.

WHAT YOU CAN LEARN FROM YOUR BAD HABITS

When you use the Inner Power Generator, listen to the wisdom of your personality units. Freud called this the wisdom of your unconscious. Personality units are pursuing individual goals by themselves. These goals fill certain needs for you. These needs are important even if you don't think they are.

Some people find it surprising and mysterious that units pursue individual goals by themselves. But really, it is the same as when the unit, which is in charge of maintaining your body's chemical balance, lets you know you need water. It communicates this to you in your feeling channel—you feel thirsty. Of course, this is a simple example. You have many complex units serving you in more complicated ways and communicating in various channels.

Furthermore, to protect themselves from interference, personality units are rather secretive. You will recall, that whenever a case was described using this technique, we never presumed to know what the unit's goal was. Conscious assumptions are often wrong.

For example, Carl thought his jealous unit had no useful intent, but was evil and trying to make him miserable. He discovered otherwise.

The same problem behavior can have different goals for different people. I know of a case where a woman discovered her jealousy's aim was to get her husband to reassure her that he loved her. Later on, I will describe the case of another woman whose jealousy was used to keep her relationship with her husband exciting.

I have also mentioned the different goals that headaches can have.

Drinking too much has been used by personality systems not only as a symbol of rebellion, but also as means of socializing, easing tension, relaxing inhibition, coping with fears, and cooling down angry feelings.

Anger can be used by a unit trying to protect you from attack, cover up fear, resist depression, avoid initmacy, or give you power to do a difficult task.

However, the reason for unit's behavior is highly individual. When you use the Power Generator to solve your problems, you may well find your responsible unit has a goal I have not mentioned or even thought of.

The point is, when trying to get a unit to change, you should not try to impose your preconceived notions about what its aim is, but find out the hidden reason from the unit itself. You often will be surprised, sometimes delightfully so; other times you might be embarrassed about having a certain goal. One forty-year-old doctor blushed to learn he was still continuing a teenage rebellion against his stuffy parents.

HOW TO USE THE INNER POWER GENERATOR #2

Step 1: Choose Your Target

To use the Power Generator to change unwanted actions, begin by identifying your target. What do you want to stop doing? Besides stopping jealousy, or smoking, you can use it to stop overeating or stop losing your temper. Also, instead of completely stopping behaviors, you can use it to do something to a lesser degree. For example, you may wish not to be so aggressive or so meek.

However, when it comes to addictions, you have to stop completely, or your habit will creep back up to your old level. The only exception I know of is eating. This is one addiction you cannot give up!

Step 2: Establish Communication with Your Unit

Having decided what you want to change about yourself (your target), go inside yourself the same way you did when you used the first version of the Power Generator. Recall vividly in three channels the last time you were feeling your conflict. Make a trigger for it so you can go back to it when you need to.

Ask the unit responsible for keeping the target behavior pattern going if it is willing to communicate with you. Notice that you are not asking anymore of it than simply to communicate with you.

Be alert for any response. You might get clear answers in the form of verbal thoughts, so you can have an internal dialogue, similar to the dialogues you can have with a friend, or the way many of us talk to ourselves. Or the unit might answer you by showing you scenes that explain its meaning. These may be memories, or they may be newly made-up events. Sometimes it might show you a static picture, such as a tableau or a photograph. Sometimes units use a combination of channels.

However, you might get a response that is not explicit, such as Carl did when his creative parts showed him colored lights. Or it might answer with an increase in the feelings you get when you have the conflict, such as more tension in certain muscles, warmth in parts of your body, or sensations in your stomach. If you get this kind of response, it is an answer. Ask the unit to increase the response for a "yes" and decrease it for a "no." Then pay attention to the answer. It will come.

Step 3: Establish Trust with Your Unit

If you get a "no" answer, reassure that system you are not trying to get rid of it, but want to help it do its job better. Since the system you are talking to is a part of you, it will know whether you mean it. If you are sincere, it will answer "yes."

Step 4: Get Clear Communication

When you have established trust with this unit, you can ask it to talk to you directly with words or show you scenes which give you its answers. It will usually comply and talk to you, as well as show you animated pictures to make its points. (Of course, if your unit is cooperative and direct, skip those steps which do not apply, and use only those you need.)

Step 5: Find Out What the Unit Is Trying To Do for You

Now you can ask this part the key question, "What are you trying to do for me?"

When one woman used the Power Generator and asked her part that made her overeat what its purpose was, it showed her a picture of her childhood. Her grandmother, with a glowing smile on her face, was giving her a slice of freshly baked, warm, pumpernickel bread with butter melting on it. In this scene, she felt loved and cared for.

The message was clear to her that eating was a way for her to feel cared about. Logical arguments that being overweight is not healthy mattered little. The unit's priorities were different. It was seeking immediate gratification and ignoring long range outcomes. A different unit was concerned about health, but it was not as strong as this one in charge of seeing to it that she felt loved.

Step 6: Involve the Unit in the Change Process

The next step is to involve the unit which is in charge of continuing the unwanted behavior. (Remember how, in the last chapter, I referred to such parts as "the boss"?) Without the boss's help, no change will take place.

Ask that unit, "If you had a better way of doing what you want, would you use it?" This is an offer it can't refuse. Who wouldn't use something better to reach its goal?

Step 7: Use Your Creative Units

When you get your "yes," thank that unit, then go inside and talk to your creative units the same way you talked to the boss. You have many systems which are able to come up with countless goal-directed behaviors. Ask these creative systems if they are willing to help you. You will almost always get a "yes." After all, their job is to create different responses for you.

Ask these units to find different ways to achieve the bosses' purpose and then choose three of their best ones and present them to you.

Step 8: Get Agreement From All Your Units

You now have four choices — the behavior the "boss" is using now, and the three new suggested behaviors. Notice that, up until now, criticism has been suspended. Go inside yourself and ask if any unit objects to these new solutions. If you get any objections, discard the one criticized. If you must get rid of them all, go back to your creative parts and get some more.

In your work up to this point, when you have at least one new solution acceptable to all your systems, fire the trigger you made in step one to reestablish contact with the boss. Ask the boss if it is willing to use the new ways in place of the old ones. Again, since it's the one running the system you want to change, its involvement is crucial. Now, it has no reason not to agree. It is still getting its way, but with behaviors acceptable to all your units.

Step 9: Make Another Trigger For Starting The New System

With its agreement to cooperate, you need to set up a trigger as a signal for the part to use its new behaviors. For Carl, his trigger was the jealous feeling. In general, it is best to use some action which occurs naturally as a trigger, like Carl's jealous feeling or, in the case of a dieter, the hand reaching for another helping.

This way, your trigger will fire automatically when you need it. This trigger can be your own action, feeling, or the sight of something or someone. One man used the sight of his wife as a trigger to switch from his serious business part to his fun loving part.

Ask the unit in charge to choose the trigger. If it cannot, you can get your creative parts to choose it. Then ask the boss to agree to use the new system whenever the trigger is fired.

You now have a new dynamic system: an acceptable substitute behavior, agreement by the unit in charge to use it, and a trigger to activate it.

Step 10: Mentally Rehearse Your New Program

The final step is mental rehearsal. As in all mental rehearsal, use three channels or more. Imagine yourself in the situations which lead up to the unwanted behavior. Carl imagined himself watching Lisa smiling and laughing with a man.

Next comes the trigger. This is followed by imagining yourself using the next agreeable behavior as a substitute for the old undesirable behavior.

Finally, allow yourself to enjoy the new you as you imagine your reprogramed behavior in various places and situations.

TEN-STEP OUTLINE OF THE INNER POWER GENERATOR #2

1. Choose the target you want to change
2. Set up communication with the unit in charge.
3. Establish trust with the unit.
4. Get clear communication.
5. Ask the unit and find out what its positive purpose is.
6. Engage the unit in the change process.
7. Use your creative units to find substitute behaviors.
8. Use only those new behaviors that all of your units agree to.
9. Set up a trigger for the new system.
10. Mentally rehearse the new system.

You do not have to complete all ten steps in one sitting. If you reach an impasse at any of the steps, you can give it a rest and time to work things out on an unconscious level. For example, it may happen that your creative units will want a day or more to think of new solutions. You can stop at this point (Step 7).

Let your creative units do their work without bothering your conscious mind. They can come up with thousands of possibilities. All you want is for them to present you with three of their best choices.

When they are ready, you can resume the Power Programmer where you left off.

Although you will never be totally free from conflict you can use this programming technique to work towards that end any time you need to.

USING THE INNER POWER GENERATOR

You can get some replies from your personality units which may puzzle you because they do not seem to be following the outline. But they are following it. Or, actually, the outline is following your personality units. The inner power generator is a true reflection of what goes on inside us.

What is surprising is that this technique fits all personalities even though everyone's personality is unique, the structure of human personality is the same, just like the basic structure of our bodies is the same. The shape and color differ of our eyes differ, but we all naturally have two of them in our heads.

When you get an unexpected response from a personality unit, all that is needed to continue is to keep the outline firmly in mind and apply a little creativity.

Here are some examples of how this can be done. The first example concerns a woman who had trouble with jealousy, like Carl did earlier. I chose this case because it will also show how a personality unit may use this same troublesome behavior, jealousy, for different reasons that need to be satisfied by different substitute behaviors. You need your own unique solutions.

This wife who wanted to stop being jealous, tried the Inner Power Generator #2. But, when she got to step five, she ran into a hitch.

With tears of disappointment in her eyes, she explained to me, "The Power Generator was working just like you said it would until I got to the part where I asked the unit that makes me jealous what it was trying to do for me. It said it wanted to get me excited.

"That's no benefit," she went on. "That's what I want to stop. Getting excited starts the arguments. I feel out of control and my husband is threatening divorce."

"All you need to do at Step 5," I explained, "is to keep on asking until you learn the positive intent—the real reason for the unit's activity. Just ignore any negative answers and persist until you get the positive one."

"Can I do this right now, so you can help me if I need it?" she asked.

"Sure, go ahead. Do it out loud so I can hear."

She stared off in space, fired her trigger to reestablish contact with the troublesome unit and spoke out loud to herself. "What are you really trying to do *for* me," she asked her unit.

"I'm getting you stirred up," she said, speaking for her unit. "No, no, what good are you supposed to be doing for me?" she asked her unit. "To end the boredom" was the answer.

Her puzzled frown deepened and then, suddenly, a smile broke out on her face. She looked at me and said, "It's trying to get excitement back in our marriage." She went on, "You know, it's right. My husband has taken me for granted during the last year."

Her personality unit was trying to save a relationship which was threatened with indifference. The wife's jealousy had certainly removed the indifference, but at the expense of creating marital strife.

She went on with the rest of the Power Generator and her creative parts suggested doing things to put fun back in the marriage.

After doing the mental rehearsal part of the program, she happily told me, "Wow, that feels terrific. I just know it's going to work." And she was right. I see her from time to time and she tells me she is not only over her jealousy, but her marriage is great. Furthermore, because her concentration is so much better, her job is running much more smoothly.

HOW A DOCTOR TRADED JUVENILE DRINKING FOR MATURE SELF-ASSERTION

Another client, who happened to be a doctor, reported a different unusual response. His creative unit replied to his request for solutions to his problem, but the doctor couldn't understand its communication.

The problem he was trying to change was his habit of getting drunk at parties and insulting people; the more status they had, the more insulting he was. This was threatening his career. His referral sources were drying up. Although an excellent neurologist, he had insulted his fellow doctors so they were no longer sending him new patients.

He reported that all of the other steps of the Power Generator worked well. The unit, which had him get drunk at parties and insult people, used words and pictures to communicate with him clearly.

A forty-year-old man, the doctor was embarrassed when he found out what getting drunk at parties was trying to do for him. It was trying to get him to be emotionally more self-reliant. Drinking and being obnoxious was a juvenile way to rebel against his controlling parents and other authority figures.

When sober, the doctor always deferred to his parents wishes.

For instance, much to the annoyance of his wife, the doctor spent every vacation with his parents because they wanted him to. He was also unusually accommodating to others in authority. This pattern was such a habit that the doctor had not realized how much he resented putting other people's wishes before his own.

This information which the doctor learned at Step 5 was an eye opener, but when he tried Step 7, he ran into a problem.

"I had asked my creative parts," he explained, "if they were willing to give me some fresh ideas on what to do instead of drinking. I got a light feeling in my chest. When I asked it to make the feeling stronger to mean "yes," my chest felt much lighter. So that means it agreed to answer.

"But when I asked for its solutions, all I got was that feeling in my chest. My chest felt lighter, but I don't know what that means," he complained.

"A good way to get clearer communication is to bridge to other channels," I explained. "Visual and verbal communication are easier for most people to understand than feelings. You can bridge from that lightness in your chest to a visual image that will talk to you. Have you done the bridging exercises and know how to bridge from one channel to another?"

He said he did.

"Let yourself feel that lightness in your chest now," I instructed. "Make it as strong as you can and then float it out in front of you. Put a face on it, any face you happen to think of. Ask it to give you the solutions you need. Watch its mouth. As you see it move, you will hear its words."

The doctor closed his eyes for a while and then looked at me to report, "I saw a face of an old, wise man who told me clearly what to do."

His creative unit suggested he respect his own wishes more and be assertive with his parents. Then he did Step 8 to check if all parts of his personality accepted this solution. Even though one of his units felt a little guilty doing this, all parts of his personality agreed. The doctor decided it was time for him to become his own person in a mature way.

He completed the rest of the Inner Power Generator #2 easily and put his new system into action.

Not only was the doctor able to enjoy himself at parties and stay sober, his wife respected him more—both for no longer making a fool of himself, and for relating to his parents and other authorities as an adult. He regained the respect of his colleagues and they resumed referring patients to him. His practice flourished once more. Also, his wife's increased respect for him helped improve their love life too.

HOW AN EXPLOSIVE LAWYER MASTERED HIS TEMPER

Dale was a lawyer with an explosive temper who ran into another rare and unexpected response. He told me he didn't even have a creative personality unit. When he searched for one, he couldn't find it.

He was using the second version of the Inner Power Generator to stop his frequent temper outbursts. Dale had poor control of his anger, and his career was suffering because he alienated clients and colleagues.

He had tried everything he knew. Counting to ten, getting plenty of rest, and taking tranquilizers didn't work. Even being fined for contempt of court did not curb his outbursts.

At Step 5 of the Power Generator, he learned that his anger was being used to express how deeply he cared. Dale was intensely committed to justice, and whenever he thought someone was being treated unfairly he became too excited. It was clear that his commitment fueled his ambition to be a good lawyer and gave his life a sense of value. But he needed a better way to champion the underdog.

However, when he tried, in Step 7, to work with his creative abilities, he could not get in touch with them.

"I guess I'm just not creative," he confided to me.

"You're more creative than you think," I replied. "Here's what to do. Simply imagine someone you know who is creative. A person whose wisdom you trust. You can make the person up, or use someone you know."

"My old professor at law school was a gem of a guy. He knew law and he knew people," Dale responded.

"Good, imagine him and let him be your creative unit. Have him give you the answers," I instructed.

Dale went home to finish the Programmer, and later told me what happened.

This image of his professor, which really was Dale's own creative unit, suggested that Dale first become friends with his angry
unit. Some of our lawyer's difficulty stemmed from his attempt to
completely stifle any angry feelings. He thought anger was just plain
wrong, but paradoxically he became angry at himself for becoming
angry. Being friends with and respecting his anger would help. Now
that he understood the positive goal of his angry feelings, he could do
this.

Second, he was to continue to champion victims with the same
gusto, but with more tact and skill. His angry feelings were good. It
was what he did with them that mattered. His anger would be the
fuel that gave him energy and drive to be exceedingly skillful and
clever at defending clients. Instead of a bull, he was to be a fox.

This new system satisfied all parts of Dale's personality: he no
longer was embarrassing himself with temper outbursts, his deep
dedication to justice had an outlet, he was being an effective attorney
and was satisfying his clients.

Dale visited me about a year later. He was overjoyed and relish-
ing a deep personal satisfaction with his work. The new system he
had programmed with the Harmony Programmer was working
beautifully. The legal community respected him as a fiercely energetic but level-headed defender and his practice was thriving.

HOW CIGARETTE SMOKING AND OVEREATING CAN NOW BECOME UNNECESSARY

A cigarette addict was surprised and amused to learn that the
reason she smoked was to fit in with groups of people.

As an insecure teen-ager, she once needed smoking to be like
her friends. But now, she had ample social skills to help her fit in with
other people. Instead of smoking, she could substitute things such as
wearing similar clothes, using appropriate language, and discussing
topics she had in common with group members.

Meg was also surprised at what her overeating was doing for
her. Remember, Meg was the woman who found out her eating
compulsion was a way of feeling love and approval—the feelings
she used to get from her grandmother.

She tapped her creative units to come up with another acceptable way to get this feeling: praising herself. (Meg was very self-critical and hadn't realized she was so harsh with herself.) When her hand reached for excess food, a personality unit told her to stop, and instead start reviewing the things she liked about herself.

These substitute behaviors worked exceedingly well. In each case, the bad habits were replaced and became unnecessary.

The system for generating personal power will help you to change successfully any bad habit, even those that have resisted prior attempts.

MAKING IT EVEN EASIER TO GO COLD TURKEY

However, when it comes to stopping addictions, like smoking and overeating, abstaining from the continual physical craving (which will eventually fade away) can be made easier by creating a trigger for persistence.

To create her trigger, our ex-smoker drew upon the persistence she used to raise her children. Nothing could dissuade her from this.

Until her craving to smoke finally died, she used this trigger like a sword to cut through temptation.

But remember, just a simple trigger won't work to stop behaviors until the purpose behind the behavior is first satisified. The best way I know of to do this is with the Inner Power Generator.

UNEXPECTED POSITIVE "SIDE EFFECTS" FROM USING INNER POWER GENERATOR #2 PROGRAMMER

It isn't unusual for clients to report that they not only achieved their change target through "programming" but that they also achieved unexpected side benefits. After completing the Inner Power Programming system, they gained better concentration, more effectiveness at work, smoother love relationships, better health, increased persuasiveness, and most important of all—a sense of inner peace.

For instance, Meg's target was to stop overeating. She succeeded and took off thirty unwanted pounds. In addition to the weight loss, her blood pressure lowered to normal, and she gained greater stamina and energy. Although these results can be attributed to being lighter, she also lost her mild stuttering problem—a positive side effect. This happy result can only be attributed to her increased inner harmony. Her stammer was probably caused by her self-criticism.

Meg was delighted at the increase in her personal power. She acted more decisively since she no longer had her little war going on with herself. She appeared more confident and people responded to her positively. As a result, Meg was promoted to a position with more responsibility, with greater prestige and higher pay.

I already mentioned the drinking doctor's improved marriage. His wife had tolerated his drunken behavior because he had so many other fine qualities. But when he stopped being obnoxious at parties and started respecting his rights with authorities, her respect for him grew and she felt more loving.

The doctor, in turn, responded more warmly to her. Little things, which they used to become annoyed at with each other and argue about, no longer upset them. Often they would laugh about it. The doctor was happy as a king with these unexpected side benefits.

You can use the Inner Power Generator #2 yourself. It has been done by countless people now. The technique can be applied to change any undesired behavior and redirect its energy to your further enhancement.

12

How To Use The New Hypnosis To Make Triggers Work Even Better for You

It may come as a surprise to you to learn that most of these modern methods of personal change, which are described in this book, were originally developed in the field hypnosis and were designed to be used on hypnotized subjects. Yet, the discovery that these techniques were so powerful that it wasn't necessary to put a client in a hypnotic trance came as a happy surprise to me.

While triggers will work *without* hypnosis, they often work even better *with* hypnosis. This book would be incomplete if it did not include techniques for using triggers *with* hypnosis.

Unfortunately, many people are afraid of using hypnosis because of the various myths created about it—mostly in novels and movies.

When one of my patients learned I was a hypnotist, she stiffened right up and wouldn't take her eyes off of me. She admitted to being frightened that I would trick her into hypnosis and make her do something she didn't want to do. Assurances that I couldn't do this, even if I wanted to, did not help her relax. She admitted, rationally, that she wanted to make changes. However, she thought being hypnotized meant loss of control and she had a deep fear of not being in control. She was blocked by one of the seven common myths that frighten people and interfere with their taking advantage of this excellent tool.

SEVEN MYTHS ABOUT HYPNOSIS—HOW MANY HAVE YOU BELIEVED?

How many of the following seven most common myths about hypnosis have you believed?

1. You are under the power of the hypnotist and he has some supernatural power. He can hypnotize you against your will and make you do things you don't want to do or make you believe something that is untrue.
2. You can remain hypnotized forever.
3. You are asleep when hypnotized.
4. There is a special hypnotized feeling. You can tell if you are hypnotized because you feel differently.
5. Being hypnotized is a sign of inferiority. The hypnotist imposes his superior will on you.
6. You will become dependent on the hypnotist and be his slave.
7. Hypnotized people are just pretending.

THE TRUTH ABOUT HYPNOSIS

Let's look at each of these myths and replace them with the truth.

Myth 1—You Are Under the Power of the Hypnotist

Being hypnotized is an exercise in exquisite cooperation between you and the hypnotist. He is only helping you hypnotize yourself. This understanding dispels many myths. The hypnotist has no mysterious magic power. He needs your cooperation. You must want to be hypnotized, and have confidence in him and willfully follow his instructions. He cannot make you do or say anything unless you want to.

During hypnosis, not only is concentration increased, but there is a special benefit called "hypersuggestibility," during which you put aside your critical attitudes and are open to suggestions for change and growth. It is this openness to uncritical acceptance of new thoughts and ideas that makes hypnosis such a powerful tool.

However, this makes many people leery. "If the hypnotist can put helpful ideas in my mind, couldn't he just as easily put harmful ones there when I have my guard down?" they ask.

This fear is based on the mistaken idea that you are being controlled by the hypnotist. But hypnosis is really a co-operative venture between subject and operator. If you analyze what is happening, you will find that the subject is actually hypnotizing himself, with the guidance of the hypnotist. The hypnotist helps him to do this just as a teacher teaches a student to learn. The actual learning is up to the student, and the student maintains control.

To illllustrate, one of my patients (let's call him "Johnny") had severe, unrelenting pain. His right leg had been crushed in an automobile accident a year before I began seeing him. He had spent six months in traction and still wore a brace. Addicted to pain-killing drugs, he was being weaned off them by substituting hypnosis as the pain killer. During one group therapy session, he went into a deep trance and experienced profound relief. But, when I hypnotized him again during this same session, I gave him a posthypnotic suggestion that, upon awakening, his back would itch and could only be relieved by my scratching it.

It didn't work. The explanation is simple. Johnny wanted relief from his pain. He was interested in that and went along willingly with all suggestions that helped him. But he did not care about becoming dependent on me to scratch his back, so he rejected that suggestion.

The protective functioning of the mind is also demonstrated when I am leading a group through a guided image, a scene that I have them imagine with much detail provided by me. I may have them imagine themselves as children diving into a crystal clear lagoon. Some subjects, not having been able to swim at that age, feel fearful. But others, equally unskilled, give themselves the ability and enjoy it immensely. Still others reorient themselves to an older age when they could swim. These are adjustments that hypnotized subjects make themselves and are not under my control as the hypnotist. Even more indicative that all hypnosis is largely self- hypnosis is the fact that most subjects respond best to *unstructured* images in which they supply the material to be imagined. For example, I may tell them to imagine a happy event in their life, and they fill in the rest.

Myth 2 — You Can Remain Hypnotized Forever

The common fear that, if the hypnotist leaves or is incapacitated, you would be left in a trance forever is completely false. During hypnosis, you can wake up any time you wish. If the hypnotist is removed for any reason, you wake up naturally. Experience with countless subjects verifies this.

On rare occasions, a different situation can happen. Although the hypnotist is present, the client will go into a deep hypnotic state and not wake up when asked.

I have had only two clients refuse to wake up after I hypnotized them. The first time this happened, it occurred with my last appointment, so I simply ignored him and went ahead with my paperwork. About half an hour later, he opened his eyes and smiled sheepishly. He admitted that he heard my request to wake up, but felt so good in the trance he didn't want to come out of it and have his enjoyment interrupted. However, he had a date with his girl friend and he aroused himself to go meet her. Apparently, euphoria is fine, but life has other rewards.

The other time when a client would not wake up, I needed my office for my next appointment. I understood that she, too, was in a euphoric state that she did not want to leave. So, to awaken her, I told her that if she did not wake up now, I would not hypnotize her again and she would never enjoy this state anymore. Her eyes popped right open.

The only time hypnotized subjects do not wake up when asked are times when they are enjoying the experience so much that they do not want it to end. Of course, they wake up when they want to.

Myth 3 — You Are Asleep When Hypnotized

Actually the term *wake up* is inaccurate because you have never been asleep or "out" in any way. What really happens is that you return to your regular state of consciousness and habitual ways of thinking. However, customary usage of the term persists from the days when hypnosis was thought to be a form of sleep, so think of "awakening" from hypnosis as simply returning from an altered state of awareness. You never pass out or become unconscious while hypnotized. It is simply that your attention is so intensely focused on your inner thoughts that you choose to ignore most external stimuli.

It is most useful to think of hypnosis as a process of focusing your attention inward on your thoughts. The more completely you do this, the deeper you are in the hypnotic state. This state, or "trance," as it is more often called, occurs at three levels: light, medium, and deep. In a light trance, concentration can be easily diverted to your surroundings. In a deep trance, you are completely absorbed in your own thoughts, ignoring everything else except the hypnotist's voice. The medium trance is somewhere between the two.

Thus, while hypnotized, concentration is increased—the opposite of sleep. Unfortunately, a nineteenth-century physician named Braid coined the term "hypnotism" from the Greek word meaning "sleep." From the outside, hypnotized subjects appear to be asleep, but their minds are actively focused on their inner thoughts.

Myth 4 — There Is a Special Hypnotized Feeling

When hypnotized, you rarely feel different enough to be able to say whether or not you are hypnotized. All you usually feel is very calm. There is always awareness even if you do not remember what happened when hypnotized. We know this because such amnesia can be lifted and you will remember everything that happened during your trance.

It is unfortunate that the common belief that there is a special "hypnotized feeling" is untrue. People expect to feel strange and different, but when they don't, they mistakenly believe they were not hypnotized and so lose faith in its ability to help them.

Myth 5 — Being Hypnotized Is a Sign of Inferiority

Another myth is that the ability to be hypnotized is a sign of a weak will or inferior intelligence. The opposite is true. People confuse the ability to respond to suggestions with the tendency to be easily fooled. Although the last is a liability, suggestibility is an asset that enables you to learn at a deep level. It takes intelligence, imagination, and some creativity.

One of the easiest men to hypnotize, that I know, is a highly educated man who owns a clinic and has twenty-seven other professionals working for him. He is also on the board of directors of a hospital and is widely respected for his sound judgment, grasp of business matters, and innovative, practical solutions to administrative problems.

Usually, the more intelligent you are, the better subject you can be. There are exceptions, of course, because other factors, such as trust and motivation, play an important part. Since all hypnosis is basically self-hypnosis, you supply the actual power with your intelligence and imagination. The hypnotist is merely a guide.

Myth 6 — You Will Become Dependent on the Hypnotist

Some people also fear becoming dependent on the hypnotist. This does not happen to any greater degree than in other helping relationships. When you need surgery, you become dependent on the hospital staff. If faced with an income tax audit, it is common to feel dependent on your tax adviser. When the problem is over, you discard your dependency. The same is true of a relationship with a hypnotist. You are dependent on him only until the problem is alleviated. Of course, with self-hypnosis you automatically remain independent.

Myth 7 — Hypnotized People Are Just Pretending

Hypnosis has sardonically been defined as two people lying to each other.

However, it is difficult to believe that a subject is lying to her surgeon and pretending she is feeling no pain as she undergoes surgery. There is a motion picture demonstrating the use of hypnosis as the only anesthetic for Cesarean surgery. During the operation, a low cervical, transverse incision was made to deliver a baby. The operation was filmed by the Upjohn Company and depicts obstetricians R. August, C. Oden, and H. Cornell, operating at Mercy Hospital in Muskegon, Michigan. During the entire delivery, the patient happily sang a hymn. The entire procedure was shown, including making the incision, mopping up the blood, and withdrawing a healthy baby girl.

This is not an isolated incident. There are other medical films showing hypnotized patients undergoing surgery; also there are many similar cases written in the medical literature.

THE PROVEN POWER OF HYPNOSIS

What makes hypnosis so intriguing is its power. We are astounded to see a hypnotized subject performing feats that seem impossible in our ordinary state of consciousness. People with intractable pain have been able to stop taking addictive medication and achieve comfort. Dental patients have stopped the flow of blood during a tooth extraction to give the dentist a clear field to work in. Then, after the job was done, they have resumed the blood flow to allow the necessary clot to form.

The Yogis of the East have done even more astounding things that can be attributed to self-hypnosis. They have amazing ability to control their "involuntary" body systems.

Modern science is discovering that the general public can gain a surprising amount of control over so called involuntary sympathetic and parasympathetic systems. Pain can be lessened or eliminated, blood flow increased to parts of the body that need it, nervous tension reduced, and many stress-related illnesses eased. After fifty years of being looked upon with fear, contempt, and skepticism, hypnosis has become respectable again. Medical science has taken a new look at this remarkable phenomenon and acceded that it is extremely useful. The American Medical Association has formally approved hypnosis as a valid medical and psychological tool.

THE TRADITIONAL APPROACH TO HYPNOSIS

Traditional hypnosis attempts to change behavior by giving direct suggestions. This is done when the subject is in a deep trance because this is when he or she is the most suggestible. The subject is told to act and feel in the desired way. The example, if you are shy and want to be more confident, suggestions would be given to "be confident." These are called "countersuggestions," because they are counter to the undesired behavior. Since nothing is done to alter the underlying problem (such as the shyness), this approach relies on achieving a deep trance as a means of making the counter-suggestions powerful enough to suppress the unwanted behavior. The impulse to act the same way is still there, creating a conflict with the new directive.

What happens is that either the countersuggestion will work or it will weaken and soon fail. If it fails, then the traditional approach is to use hypno-analysis to uncover the root of the problem and resolve it. This takes considerable therapeutic skill, but is usually shorter than nonhypnotic analysis.

These older methods I have just described will not work with self-hypnosis. Hypno-analysis requires rigorous training, and counter-suggestions require a deep trance. Profound trances are seldom achieved with self-hypnosis. But even if you could hypnotize yourself deeply enough, you would have an insoluble dilemma: the attempt to direct yourself with suggestions would bring you into a lighter state. As a result, traditional self-hypnosis is limited to reinforcing suggestions given to you by a hypnotist, and to achieving deep relaxation.

THE ADVANTAGE OF THE "NEW HYPNOSIS" APPROACH

You no longer have to have a hypnotist to produce profound change. You can do it yourself by using a modern hypnotic approach. This approach is different enough to be called the "New Hypnosis."

The New Hypnosis, as opposed to the traditional approach, is based on the understanding that hypnosis is not something that is done to you. Hypnosis is something you do yourself, sometimes with the help and guidance of a hypnotist. In a basic sense, all hypnosis is self-hypnosis.

The New Hypnosis uses the trigger techniques described in this book. Because these techniques are so powerful, you can achieve the changes you need when in a light trance. Such a trance is easily achieved with self-hypnosis.

To use the New Hypnosis, apply these techniques either when you are in a self-induced trance, or when you are in the posthypnotic state immediately after awakening. When you are in a posthypnotic state, you are still hypersuggestible, and yet you have the resources of your conscious mind to guide you. You can follow the instructions which are given for the trigger technique you are using. This circumvents the problem with traditional hypnosis, where you need an outside hypnotist to induce a deep trance and give you countersuggestions.

With self-hypnosis, you have the convenience and privacy of your own home. Also, self-hypnosis enables you to use hypnosis more frequently than if you had to travel to see a hypnotist. This is especially helpful when using it to reduce the effects of stress, where you should hypnotize yourself every day.

IF YOU CAN READ THIS PAGE, YOU CAN HYPNOTIZE YOURSELF

If you can read this page, you can hypnotize yourself. Your ability to extract meaning from words, while ignoring insignificant distractions, are the minimum skills needed.

You probably have more then the minimum skills. If you can think in more than one channel (and by now, if you have practiced the exercises presented earlier in the book, you most certainly can), you can hypnotize yourself.

The next requirement for successful hypnosis is desire. The more you want to be hypnotized, the more successful you will be at it. Want it to happen and it will happen. Even pain will not distract you, if you use it to motivate yourself. Also, desire will help you put the time and effort you need into it. Like any skill, self-hypnosis improves with practice.

Hypnosis requires intelligence. Retarded, senile, confused, or inattentive people cannot use it. Along with intelligence goes concentration—the ability to think of one thing at a time. Concentration is to the mind what strength is to the muscle. The more weight a muscle can lift, the stronger it is considered to be. The longer your mind can steadily focus on an idea, the stronger it is. Hypnosis is the ability to keep on focusing your thoughts on your mental channels.

However, intelligent people with ordinarily good powers can have their concentration interfered with. Fear and skepticism are the most common ways you can be distracted from hypnosis. This is because, if you are thinking about your fears while hypnotizing yourself, your attention is divided between two things and you are not concentrating on a single idea.

The same is true of skepticism. If you are telling yourself it can't work or wondering if it is working, you are dividing your concentration. The best antidote for skepticism is belief. Simply believe with all your mind that it will work, and it will.

Another way you can interfere with being hypnotized is to analyze what is happening at the time. I used to be a poor subject for hypnosis because I kept dividing my attention by analyzing the hypnotist's's technique and making mental notes on what things I wanted to remember to use myself. When I gave this up, I became a good subject.

You are more adept at self-hypnosis than you realize, having experienced many naturally occurring trance states. Practically everyone has stared into a fire, watching the flickering flames caress the logs. There is a certain rhythm to the dance of the flames, but their movements are completely random. The colors are bright and make subtle shifts in shade and hue. Reds blend into yellows and oranges. Sometimes a stray green or blue will briefly appear and then fade away, almost shyly. As you continue to gaze, you probably are not aware, until later, that you feel very restful, your mind at peace. In the midst of your contemplation, the rest of the world fades away and it takes a fairly strong intrusion to gain your attention. This fascination may last for a few brief seconds or go on for hours.

An ordinary experience, but your state of consciousness was altered. Most likely you wouldn't realize it, but you were hypnotized into what is termed a "medium trance." This is all a trance is—not so strange and mysterious after all.

Or have you ever had the experience of getting into your car and driving to a familiar place and after your arrival, realizing that all you can remember is turning onto the highway and then, many miles later, pulling into your parking place? All the rest is a blank. Yet you know you have negotiated traffic, stopped for red lights, started up again when the lights turned green, pulled in and out of lanes, and performed all the other maneuvers that had to be done correctly and safely. Your unconscious mind did it gracefully and probably even better without your conscious awareness interfering. This is a common example of a hypnotic state with amnesia, which is considered a deep trance phenomenon.

Or recall those times when you are walking through the woods on a soft summer's day, enjoying the stately array of tree trunks. They are similar and yet you can see subtle differences in color and texture. As your eyes follow a tree trunk upward, you are fascinated by the intricate branching of the limbs into smaller and smaller twigs, while the patterned leaves filter the sunlight into a yellow-green vaulted cathedral ceiling. Closing your eyes, you can hear the quiet symphony of singing insects, and note a persistent high whine, punctuated by the rhythmic croaking of the frogs. At the same time, some birds chirp back and forth. That feeling of oneness with nature and with yourself is a common altered state of consciousness induced by hypnosis.

You can now realize a trance is not something "far out." You are not zonked into being a zombie or anything like that. You are conscious. The previous example of watching a fire, driving a car, and walking through the woods are natural hypnotic inductions that result in a trance. That is what a trance feels like. It is an inward concentration, during which you pay close attention to your thoughts, instead of your surroundings. It is much like when you are reading an absorbing book. If something happens around you that requires your attention, you can easily shift your attention to deal with it.

Now that you realize how masterful you already are at self-hypnosis, you can learn how to use it to enhance your life and get to the fun things about the New Hypnosis—solving problems. If you get enjoyment from solving puzzles—jigsaw, crossword, Rubik's Cube, or whatever—imagine what a thrill it will be to solve a personal puzzle, freeing yourself from a psychological block and enabling yourself to realize your full potential.

Self-hypnosis is a two-part procedure: induction and utilization. Induction refers to the methods used to hypnotize yourself. Utilization is using techniques to achieve the changes you want. Once you have induced a trance in yourself, you will be able to use the methods described earlier to obtain your specific goals.

HOW TO HYPNOTIZE YOURSELF

There are many methods for inducing self-hypnosis. Hundreds have been described in various books and journals. But all you need to understand is that practically all hypnotic methods rely on a common principle: They are simply means of leading you to focus your attention on your inner thoughts. This is most effectively accomplished by leading yourself to think with your sensory channels. For example, when you follow directions that have you imagine a fire, seeing it in your mind's eye uses your visual channel. Listening to the imaginary logs snap and crackle uses your hearing channel. And sensing the fire heat your body uses your feeling channel. From one to all five channels can be involved.

The more channels you are able to imagine with, the better subject you can be. This understanding will be helpful to us for designing self-hypnotic induction methods using multichannels.

How to use your channels is all worked out for you in the following directions for self-hypnosis, so you won't have to think about it, but will do it automatically.

The use of external gadgets, such as pendulums, metronomes, white noise, and flashing lights is of little value. It is much more effective to imagine something.

You may do better with one type of self-hypnotic method than another. I will describe a sample of each type, with step-by-step procedures, including outlines for you to follow. Although I will give you several reliable induction methods, you really only need one. But it is useful to know of others, if you get bored. More importantly, because of your own needs, certain ones may work better than others for you. Try them all and find those that you are most successful with.

All the following methods of self-hypnosis start with you sitting or lying down comfortably. Do not analyze or try to figure out what is happening. Save that for afterwards. If you find yourself falling asleep, you, of course, won't be able to go ahead with the utilization methods for achieving your goals. (Unless your goal is simple stress reduction. In that case, falling asleep would be fine.) If you want to prevent falling asleep, just hold your tongue lightly against the roof of your mouth during self-hypnosis.

EASY AND SAFE INDUCTION METHODS

Induction Method #1

Let us start with a simple, but effective, induction method. It engages your verbal channel. Close your eyes or, if you prefer, gaze at a spot on the far wall. Take three deep breaths, then start counting backwards from fifty down to zero. With each number, you will go deeper into a comfortable, relaxed state. By the time you get to zero, you will be in a trance. To come out of it, count forwarded to fifty. At fifty, you will be wide awake, refreshed, and alert. If you want to go even deeper, repeat the counting backwards process. All you do is count backward from fifty to zero. You will know you are deep enough when you feel relaxed and peaceful, with little or nothing else on your mind.

Outline For Induction Method #1

1. Close your eyes, or gaze at a spot.
2. Take three deep breaths.
3. Slowly count backwards from fifty to zero.
4. Count back to fifty to awaken.
5. Repeat if necessary.

Induction Method #2

Another induction method which engages your sound channel involves staring at a spot above eye level, closing your eyes and repeating the word "one" to yourself with each breath until you feel in a dreamy state. Take about ten or twenty minutes. Try to exclude extraneous thoughts. If they intrude, patiently and graciously bring yourself back to thinking "one." To awaken, count to five and you will be alert, wide awake and refreshed.

A simple variation is to simply repeat the word "one" to yourself without consciously coordinating it with your breathing.

Outline For Induction Method #2

1. Stare at a spot.
2. Close your eyes.
3. Repeat "one" for twenty or thirty minutes.
4. Count to five to awaken.

This method is similar to a form of meditation in which a mantra is said over and over. Many, if not all, of the same benefits derived

from meditation are also derived from simply inducing self-hypnosis. If you are a meditator, you can use meditation for a self-hypnotic induction.

If you don't like numbers, you can create your own version of an
auditory channel induction. Imagine listening to some sound like surf
hitting a rocky shore, music, or repeating, inside your head, a favorite
word like "serenity." Using your imagination instead of an outside
source, such as a rcording, is better. You will go deeper.

Induction Method #3

For another induction, close your eyes and imagine all the tension in your upper body draining out through your finger tips, like
water flowing out of a faucet and forming a puddle on the floor. Then
imagine all the tension in the lower part of your body draining out
through your toes. Continue feeling all the tension draining out of
your entire body, as that puddle on the floor gets bigger and bigger.
Notice your muscles; find a tense one and tighten it even more. Hold
it tightly for a few seconds until it feels tired and then let go. Do this
for each tense muscle that you find. You may find none, or your may
find several. After tensing and relaxing those you find, continue to
feel all the tension drain out from your body through your fingers
and toes. Do this for ten to twenty minutes and then count to five to
awaken, feeling alert and full of energy.

Induction Method #4

Another good technique is to use your visual channel and imagine something beautiful. Some people think of a sunset at the sea-
shore, others like imagining a burning log. Think of something you
enjoy. The procedure is simple. Close your eyes and see your picture
brightly, clearly and in detail. Spend about fifteen to thirty minutes,
then awaken yourself by counting to five.

Induction Method #5

Since you will probably do best using more than one channel,
the following self hypnotic method uses all five channels. You will
recognize the bridging technique is used.

Begin by imagining an enjoyable scene and see it like I described in the paragraph above. Then hear the sounds in it, feel the sensations. You can even add smell and taste. For example, after you are seated comfortably with your eyes closed (if you like), picture a beautiful lagoon. It is crystal clear, and so still it reflects the blue sky and the trees that surround it. As you watch, its surface begins to ripple and the leaves flutter in the wind so that you can hear their rustle and feel the wind caress your face and ruffle your hair. The wind brings the scent of your favorite flower. After filling your nostrils with this aroma, you bend over the pool and drink its fresh cool water. When you are ready, awaken by counting to five.

Doing this with your favorite fantasy is a great induction technique. Here are the steps for imagining something using all your sensory channels. Spend ten to thirty minutes doing this.

Outline for Induction Method #5

1. Close your eyes.
2. See the scene clear and bright.
3. Hear the sounds in it.
4. Feel the temperature in your surroundings.
5. Smell any fragrance.
6. Taste something in your scene.
7. Awaken by counting to five.

Induction Method #6

This method is one of my favorites and it is very effective. Stare at a single interesting object and name to yourself three things you are seeing. For instance, you might say, "Now I see the radio dial. I see the light shining off its chrome sides. I see the dial's black center." Now, remark on three things you are hearing. "I hear the sound of voices drifting in from the other room. I hear the fan. I hear the traffic from the road." Then make three comments about what you are feeling. "I feel my feet on the floor. I feel the texture of the slacks beneath my hands. I feel my eyes blink." Up to this point, you have made three statements about what you saw, three about what you heard, and three about what you felt. Now, preferably using different statements, make two about what you see, two about what you hear, and two about what you feel. Then go through it once more, making one statement each about what you see, hear, and feel.

Your eyes will probably get drowsy long before you finish. If so, close them and substitute imaginary sights, while still using input from your surroundings for things to hear and feel.

Steps for the See, Hear, and Feel Self-Hypnosis Technique

1. Look at an object.
2. Say three things you see.
3. Say three things you hear.
4. Say three things you feel.
5. Say two things you see.
6. Say two things you hear.
7. Say two things you feel.
8. Say one thing you see.
9. Say one thing you hear.
10. Say one thing you feel.
11. Awaken by counting to five.

In addition to trying these self-hypnosis techniques to find which one works best for you, you may, if you wish, combine some of them. For example, you might start with counting backwards, switch to an enjoyable imaginary scene, and finish the session with feeling the tension drain out of your fingers and toes.

You will find all these techniques pleasant. While you are hypnotized, you will be able to respond to and take care of important interruptions whenever necessary. It is better to find someplace where such disturbances are at a minimum. But if you are interrupted during a self-hypnotic procedure, you can awaken to attend to the problem, and then return to your induction. You will find yourself going even deeper when you resume after a brief interruption. Hypnotists sometimes do this purposely to deepen a trance. They will awaken a subject for a few seconds during an induction and then resume the hypnosis. This procedure is called "fractionization."

A Simple Safeguard

If you have any traumatic memories, it is possible to relive them vividly when hypnotized and become unnecessarily upset.

To avoid this, do not explore your past without proper preparation. When you first hypnotize yourself, use only pleasant, enjoyable images. Later, if you have any troublesome memories, you can take care of them with the Triple Split Technique, as explained in Chapter 7.

HOW TO MAKE TRIGGERS MORE POWERFUL WITH THE NEW SELF-HYPNOSIS

First, practice hypnotizing yourself a few times until you feel comfortable with it. Then, simply select the appropriate Trigger technique for achieving the outcome you want and use it in conjunction with self-hypnosis. First read over the instructions on the technique you want to use, such as the Triple Split Technique, or the Fast and Easy Method for erasing unreasonable fears. Next, use your favorite induction to go into a trance. Then follow the instructions.

If you need to open your eyes to read the instructions again or look at your notes, you can. You will still have the benefits of hypnosis because you will be in the posthypnotic state right after waking from hypnosis and still suggestible. Also, you can close your eyes again and continue under hypnosis. (remember fractionization?)

Most of you will find the Trigger techniques work better when combined with self-hypnosis. You are more suggestible when hypnotized because hypnosis produces several effects: images are more intense and clear, outside distractions are ignored owing to increased concentration, and a deep feeling of calmness — even euphoria — is achieved.

For instance, one woman I worked with desperately wanted to get over her illness and tried mental healing imagery to enhance her medical treatment. At first, she used imagery without hypnosis and gained modest improvement. When she used the same technique under hypnosis, her images were stronger and she began healing more quickly. She soon recovered completely.

Similarly, the actor, described in an earlier chapter who used the New Behavior Programmer to improve his acting, found he got better results when he practiced while hypnotized.

A college student had trouble installing the learning trigger techniques because he was distracted so easily. Since hypnosis so effectively focuses attention inward, away from outside stimuli, self-hypnosis was ideal for this young man. He responded well to induction #5, the "See, Hear, and Feel Method." This induction method suited the student because if fit in with his personality. He was easily distracted because he was so attuned to outside stimuli. The induction method starts by directing attention to outside stimuli and gradually narrows the focus inward.

With hypnosis, the student successfully installed each of the learning triggers and mastered the technique.

Because he was hypnotized when he built his learning trigger, he goes into a hypnotic state each time he fires it. This produces profound concentration and is in no way a problem. To an observer he appears only to be thinking deeply. When necessary, he can respond instantly to an important outside matter which needs his attention.

He went on to be an excellent student and won a much needed scholarship. His friends were impressed with his new ability to concentrate so well.

The trigger methods for erasing unreasonable fears usually work better with hypnosis because hypnosis automatically produces feelings of tranquility—sometimes euphoria. These feelings water down fears.

Also, the Triple Split Technique benefits greatly from the sense of peace you feel when hypnotized. This peaceful feeling helps dilute the pain in traumatic memories.

My clinical experience, and that of my colleagues, is that trigger techniques work extremely well and combining them with hypnosis usually makes them even more potent.

With or without hypnosis, triggers are extremely powerful and effective. Use your ingenuity. Put triggers to work for you to change your life.

References

W. Ross Ashby, M.A., M.D., D.P.M., *Design for a Brain* (London: Science Paperbacks, Chapman and Hall, Ltd., 1952).

W. Ross Ashby, M.A., M.D., D.P.M., *Introduction to Cybernetics* (London: Chapman and Hall, Ltd., 1952).

R. Assagioli, *Psychosynthesis* (New York: Dorman & Co., 1965).

T. X. Barber, "Measuring 'Hypnotic-like' Suggestibility With and Without 'Hypnotic Induction,' etc.," *Psych. Reports*, 16 (1965), 809-44.

Eric Berne, *Games People Play* (New York: Grove Press, 1964).

Eric Berne, *Transactional Analysis in Psychotherapy* (New York: Grove Press, 1961).

Eric Berne, *Sex in Human Loving* (New York: Simon & Shuster, 1970).

Eric Berne, *What Do You Say After You Say Hello?* (New York: Grove Press, 1972).

Adelaide Bry, *Visualization: Directing the Movies of Your Mind* (New York: Barnes & Noble Books, 1972).

Hedges Capers and Glen Holland, "Stroke Survival Quotient." *Transactional Analysis Journal*, I, 3 (1971):40.

J. R. Cautela, "Covert Sensitization." *Psychological Reports*, 74 (1967) 459–68.

Noam Chomsky, Massachusetts Institute of Technology, *Language and the Brain* (New York: Harcourt Brace Jovonovich, Inc., 1968).

T. A. Clawson, R. H. Swader, "The Hypnotic Control of Blood Flow and Pain: etc.", *Amer. J. Clin. Hypnosis*, 17 (1975) 168–69.

Patricia Crossman, "Permission and Protection," *Transactional Analysis Bulletin* 5, 19 (1961), 152–53.

G. C. Curtis, "Sensory Experiences During Treatment of Phobias by *in vivo* Exposure, "*Am. J. Psychiatry*, 138.8 (Aug. 1981) 1095–97.

Dwight Deyoung, "A Comparison of Five Methods of Mental Practice in the Improvement and Retention of Perceptual Motor Skill," *Dis. Abs. Int.*, 40(3-A) (1979), 1354–55.

M. C. Diamond, "The Aging Brain: Some Enlightening and Optimistic Results," *Am. Sci.*, (1978) Jan.–Feb.: 68(1), 1969–71.

M. C. Diamond, "Effects of Environmental Enrichment and Impoverishment on Rat Cerebral Cortex," *J. Neurob.*, 3(1) (1972), 47–64.

Marlene R. Eisen and Erika Fromm, "The Clinical Use of Self-Hypnosis in Hypnotherapy: Tapping the Functions of Imagery and Adaptive Regression," *Int. J. Clin. Exp. Hypnosis*, 31(4) (1983), 243–55.

E. Fromm, et al, "The Phenomena and Characteristics of Self-Hypnosis," *Int. J. Clin. Exp. Hypnosis*, 29 (1981), 189–246.

W. Timothy Gallwey, *The Inner Game of Tennis*, (New York: Random House, 1974).

Robert L. Goulding, and Mary McClure Goulding, *The Power Is in the Patient*, (San Francisco, Calif.: TA Press, 1978).

J. R. Hilgard, "Imaginative Involvement: Some Characteristics of the Highly Hypnotizable and the Non-Hypnotizable," *Int. J. Clin. Exp. Hypnosis*, 22 (1974), 138–156.

Edmond Jacobson, *Progressive Relaxation*, (Chicago: University of Chicago Press, 1942).

Murial James and Dorothy Jongward, *Born to Win* (Reading, Mass.: Addison-Wesley, 1971).

Stephen R. Lankton, *Practical Magic* (Cupertino, Calif.: Meta Publications, 1980).

M. S. Lindaur, "Imagery and Sensory Modality," *Percep. Mot. Skills,* 29 (1969), pp 203–15.

A. Maslow, "Neurosis as a Failure of Personal Growth," *Humanitas,* 3 (1967) 153–69.

Maxwell Maltz, *Psycho-Cybernetics* (Englewood Cliffs, N.J.: Prentice-Hall, Inc., 1960).

A. W. Meyers, R. Schleser, T. M. Okwumabua, Memphis State U., "A Cognitive Behavioral Intervention for Improving Basketball Performance," *Res. Q. Exercise & Sport,* 53(4) (Dec. 1982) 344–47.

Michael Murphy, *Golf in the Kingdom* (New York: Dell 1973).

U. Neisser, "The Process of Vision," *Scientific American* 219(3) (Sept. 1968) 204–14.

U. Neisser and G. Nigro, *Psychology Today* 17 (May 1983), 60.

G. Nigro, "Improvement of Skill Through Observation and Mental Practice," *Dis. Abs. Internat.,* 44(9-B) (Mar. 1984), 54307.

W. Penfield, "Memory Mechanisms," *Arch. Neurol. & Psychiatry,* 67 (1952) 178–98.

Fritz S. Perls, *Gestalt Therapy Verbatim* (Lafayette, Calif.: Real People Press, 1969).

Karl H. Pribram, Stanford University, *Languages of the Brain* (Monterey, Calif.: Brooks/Cole Publishing Co., 1971).

A. Richardson, "Voluntary Control of the Memory Images," *The Nature and Function of Imagery,* ed. P. W. Sheenan (New York: Academic Press, 1972).

Carl R. Rogers, *On Becoming a Person* (Boston: Houghton Miffin Co., 1961).

Julian B. Rotter, "Social Learning Psychotherapy," in *Psychopathology Today,* 3rd. ed., ed. William S. Sahakian (Tasca, Ill.: F. E. Peacock, Publishers, Inc., 1970), pp 541–46.

Michael Rutter et al., *Fifteen Thousand Hours: Secondary Schools and their Effect on Children* (Cambridge: Harvard University Press 1979).

Virginia Satir, *People Making* (Palo Alto, Calif.: Science and Behavior Books, 1972).

A. W. Schiff and J. L. Schiff, "Passivity," *Transactional Analysis Journal*, I, 1 (1971), 71–78.

J. M. Silva, "Competitive Sport Environments: Performance Enchancement Through Cognitive Intervention," *Behavior Modification*, 6 (4) (1982), 443–63.

O. Carl Simonton and Stephanie Matthews-Simonton, *Getting Well Again* (New York: J. P. Tarcher, 1978).

N. P. Spanos, H. L. Radtke-Bodorik, J. F. Ferguson, and B. Jones, "The Effects of Hypnotic Susceptibility, Suggestions for Analgesia, and the Utilization of Cognitive Strategies on the Reduction of Pain," *J. Abnorm. Psychology*, 88(3) (1979), 282–92.

Rene Spitz, "Hospitalism, Genesis of Psychiatric Conditions in Early Childhood." *Psychoanalytic Study of the Child*, 1 (1945), 53–74.

G. Stacher, P. Schuster, P. Bauer, R. Lahoda, and D. Schulze, "Effects of Relaxation or Analgesia on Pain Threshold and Pain Tolerance in the Waking and in the Hypnotic State," *J. Psychosomatic Res.* 19 (1975) 259–65.

T. G. Stampfl and D. J. Levis, "Essentials of Implosive Therapy; etc.," *Journal of Abnormal Psychology*, 72 (1967) 496–503.

J. Taylor, "The Effects of Mental Fitness on Athletic Performance," *Int. J. Sport Psychol.*, 12(2) (1981), 87–95.

D. Van Nuys, "Meditation, Attention, and Hypnotic Susceptibility: A Correlation Study," *Int. J. Clin. Exp. Hypnosis*, 21 (1973), 59–69.

N. Weinberger, "Epinephrine Enables Pavlovian Fear Conditioning under Anesthesia,"*Science* 223 (F 10 '84) 605–7.

Jerome D. White and Terri White, *Self-Fulfilling Prophecies in the Inner City* (Chicago: Illinois Institute of Applied Psychology, 1970).

K. D. White, R. Ashton, S. Lewis, University of Queensland, "Learning a Complex Task: Effects of Mental Practice, Physical Practice, and Imagery Ability," *Int. J. Sport Psychol.*, 10(2) 1979, 71–78.

S. Williams, G. Dooseman, and Erin Kleifield, "Comparative Effectiveness of Guided Mastery and Exposure Treatments for Intractable Phobias," *J. Cons. Clin. Psychol.* 52(4), 1984, 505–18.

S. Wiseman and U. Neisser, "Perceptual Organization as a Determinant of Visual Recognition Memory," *S. Amer. J. Psychology* 87(4) (Dec. 1974), 675–81.

Joseph Wolpe, *The Practice of Behavior Therapy.* (New York: Pergamon, 1969).

Joseph Wolpe and Arnold Lazuras, *Behavior Therapy Techniques* (New York: Pergamon Press, 1966).

Index